I AM THE WOLF

I AM THE WOLF

Anthony Michael

VANTAGE PRESS
New York

Published by Vantage Press, Inc.
516 West 34th Street, New York, New York 10001

Manufactured in the United States of America
ISBN: 0-533-10396-7

Library of Congress Catalog Card No.: 92-96828

0 9 8 7 6 5 4 3 2

For Gordon and Charmaine

Contents

Foreword

These days all people are seeking knowledge whether they wish to admit it or not; knowledge, but not wisdom. Wisdom to most people is something that is unattainable so not much thought is given to the topic.

Knowledge is things of the past and is something that is attainable by everyone who cares enough to consider it. Hindsight always comes too late; this is a given. But wisdom? Wisdom is of the future and is available only by special favor.

Charmaine

From the Author

Much wisdom was revealed during the sixties, seventies, and eighties from some great minds and some not so great but, nevertheless, wisdom. I call it wisdom because many of the things people said came true in some form or another. The problem with much of the wisdom, as it was spoken or written, was that it was not disseminated in a form that would peak everyone's interest and also cause complete understanding of what the author was trying to convey. I don't like to say that the wisdom was wasted because I don't want to see that happen to the wisdom contained in this book, but it was wasted.

The writings contained within these pages are the thoughts and wisdom of an Indian medicine man who has roots that date back to the beginning of time. His current name is Standing Wolf; he is spirit and I am his incarnate.

The words of Standing Wolf came to me in many ways, in dreams, in visits, through automatic writing, and through a computer. The ability of this wise man to convey his messages in these ways was astounding, even frightful. Many times I chose not to believe what I was hearing, writing, reading, and seeing. I was not a seeker, I was not a walk-in, I was not into anything metaphysical, and I do not believe this to be a metaphysical experience.

I believed that I lived a normal life, as far as you can interpret the word normal, until my first visit from Standing Wolf. I would not say that my experiences with Standing Wolf changed my life permanently but, certainly, temporarily. I had tried desperately to block Standing Wolf out and at times I had thought I was successful. But the words this man was sending to me were so profound, so wise, and so desperately needed today, the only thing I could do was surrender, meet his challenges, and get it over with so that I could get on with my life; this writing allows me to finish with it, or so I believe.

The results culminated in traveling, personal experiences, conversations, dreams, writings, and more, all with an Indian man whom I have doubted, insulted, joked about, and laughed at and whom I have not seen since he intervened in what I believed was an attempt to take my life in South America on July 11, 1991.

Try as I did to make him go away, he kept coming back, more profound each time. My only surprise is that I was able to continue with my life after experiences that would have sent most into permanent seclusion or prolonged paranormal shock. I attribute my revival to a keen sense of humor, and the fact that I have been described by many as someone whose elevator does not quite go to the top floor; it stops at the mouth before ever reaching the brain. This description stems from my sense of humor. I have always been a firm believer that a joke, a laugh, a smile, and cutting wit can make things right in my world—believe me, they do.

Standing Wolf was not a visionary, as I had originally thought. In fact, I now believe him to have been an entity, an entity who has traveled into the past and into the future; traveling freely throughout his and other lifetimes past, present, and yet to come; and who has brought the knowledge and wisdom of his journeys to the present.

Because of the knowledge and the wisdom he attained, he was able to put the two together and disseminate to me in the present that which we all need to know if we are ever going to make it in life. The only thing I have yet to figure out is the age-old question we have all asked ourselves at least once in our lifetime: Why me? Why is he dumping all this mess on me?

I have enough problems of my own. I am no different than any other in that I would like to have all the answers. But what if we did have all the answers? How would we react? Would we go insane from the sheer simplistic beauty of all the answers?

Well, my friends, we won't go insane. We may drink a little more, cuss a little more, and introvert our personalities slightly as a form of self-preservation, protection if you will, but we will not go insane. Besides, it would be like taking a trip somewhere that we found profusely boring; once would be enough. Why go insane when, for the most part, all of us have already been there? So if you'll pardon me while I take a fist full of lithium, then we'll get on with it.

Again, why Standing Wolf chose me to bestow his wisdom upon is a question I have tangled with for many months. I am thankful for Charmaine, the best sounding board I have ever found. I could scream, bitch, and holler until I was blue in the face (or eyes), and she took it all like a trooper, offering advice, food for thought, and solace. I was not going insane; and although it was never a topic of discussion, Charmaine made me see that. It was painful to reveal to her some months later that she was a stagnate soul. I thought for sure I knew better, but perhaps not. We all have a role and hers was to be a rational, clear-headed sounding board for a young man in massive confusion.

I looked for a credibility gap, but I am nobody. I have not made a name for myself in the field of what we refer to as paranormal, so the credibility is not there. The only reason that could possibly hold any key would be innocence. My mind had not been plagued with metaphysical writings or interest. I was totally new to the idea. I am educated, intelligent, and, most of all, objective. I accept nothing at its face value and question just about everything. For someone such as me to surrender to the experience recounted in the following pages, then to compile all of it into a book and actually publish it for others to share is, in itself, for me an incredible feat.

As you turn these pages, you will see what the innocence has wrought. You will share the fear of confrontation, the joy of realization, and the sheer bliss of finding out for sure that this is not all there is, that tomorrow will come. If not on this Earth and in this lifetime, certainly somewhere else. The Grand Creation is not a myth, but by the same token Darwin was not completely nuts either. The big bang theory has credibility; hell, it has reality.

I trust that the same objectivity that I possess is in all of us. Readers will reap from these pages what is necessary for them to understand not only who they are but where they are headed and where they have been. Also, to understand that our time here is temporary until we move on, and we do move on. You will come to know that there is no death, only continued existence, and a changing of worlds.

Some of what is contained in these pages may not be pleasing to all. There are thoughts on disease, religion, government, medical technology, and more. You must certainly have wondered how disease was cured before modern technology came along. It is also necessary to remember that along with modern technology came diseases that were previously unknown. I am a firm believer that man creates nearly all of his own diseases.

There are thoughts on starvation, procreation, sexual preferences, and even messages about how wrong we have been regarding life on other planets. Some of the revelations you may not like. But the revelations are so simple they are astounding.

The chapter "Chronicles" was a period during which I was allowed to ask any question of Standing Wolf, and "we" would answer. Imagine having the opportunity to ask someone who truly had the answers to any questions you wanted. Would the questions flow from your mind easily? It is hard to be put on the spot, so to speak, in that manner. I think I asked some good questions, things that were of interest to me or things others suggested to me, but I'll bet you could think of many more. The answers are in understandable terms and are so simplistic it will amaze everyone that we hadn't thought of them ourselves.

So many times we have heard the expression "the miracle of life." Well, I have come to learn that life is not a miracle. Life is a gift and there is reason for life. Everyone has a purpose, and I hope these writings will enable you to know what your purpose is. If not, my hope is that they will at least point you in the right direction in finding your purpose because, believe me, there is one and it is out there.

Turn the pages and greet the Wolf, for he is the most kind, the most blunt, the most loving, and the most intelligent being I have ever encountered, and it truly breaks my heart that his presence in my life was so short.

Acknowledgments

The author wishes to acknowledge the following individuals for their contributions and input:

Charmaine, to whom these writings are dedicated. Your compassionate thirst for knowledge and your ability to accept all that you hear as factual, simply because it has a source, are true and rare gifts. Thank you for the guiding hand, the caring heart, and the unbending ear.

Gordon, to whom these writings are also dedicated. Thank you for your assistance on "Mother Earth, the Healer." Thank you for the freedom you extend by never questioning what I do, think, or say and always being supportive in my endeavors. You have captured a special place in the heart of this Wolf, and you may always call it home. *On to the next Crusade!*

Finally, Standing Wolf, whoever you were, whoever you are, and whoever you will be . . . Thank you for the love, the caring heart, and for leading my team. I will never forget.

The Wolf

As If There Need Be a Reason . . .

All are my children; all are of the same root. There truly is no color, no race, no nationality when you look at the heart, only the oneness that was the beginning and will be the endurance until this all ends, but group yourselves as you may and try to be at peace with such misgivings.

Be at peace with one another; strike up the harmony that is there; call upon it now, for the day will near when you shall need one another and there will be no time for questions, no time for reconciliations, no time for if. No time for soul searching, no time to seek the answers because it will be too late and in their finding you will inherit despair.

Remember, when the bird lands, he rests, he is dormant, he seeks nothing; but when he flies, he is fulfilling a goal. Do not be dormant, children of the land, for while you rest the wisdom of the land will continue to unfold around you, without you. If nothing else, be a part of your own existence, be prepared, care about the future time that will come after you for the final ending will be truly hateful, truly wicked, and as a remorse that you could never voluntarily experience but will be forced to.

Take the blinds from in front of your eyes and see the hand that is reaching out to you for your own benevolence. Remove your hearts from their sheltered prisons for they thirst and their parched conditions will require much to quench. Seek it, see it, attain it, be the commander of the supreme gift, that which was given you without asking, that which is yours and yours alone; it is life.

I will know the time and I will send him in confusion. I will send him in thirst and I will send him with pity, remorse, and a genuine tear.

You will know him, for his words will be unlike his own. You will know him, for his actions will be unlike his own. You will know him, for he will touch your heart and awaken its tender feelings. The innocence will be the victor in this manner.

He will do great things for many, but he will not realize it until it has already happened. The great things will be more of an awakening, a realization that the spoken words and the written words bear value and meaning worth taking to heart. His name will be placed upon the words of another.

And the final message: dare we not to question its meaning, dare we not to ignore it either . . .

Behold, the beginning of the final days, the days when my children will question my ways, perhaps scoff at the meaning of the Grand Creation. I will open my forgiving heart and send forth my son . . . and the white man will come.

Lojon

Introduction: From Chief Two-Pines (1742–1869)

I think to myself that this is a child, this Wolf: But who am I to question "his" judgment. I watched a travesty unfold before my undying eyes as this child was put through what certainly must have been a test of courage, a test of strength, a test of intelligence, and the hardest test of all, a test of his self-being.

I watched the tears, I watched the laughter, and I watched him fall time and time again, only to keep getting up. Such a fool this Wolf. But is he? The seed was planted as a child and the seed remained a child. Is it any wonder he grieved so easily? A child does not understand. What does a child do when he does not understand . . . ? He questions. He can become a nuisance he questions so much. Oftentimes I laughed at the innocence but was shamed in the face of his childlike pride.

In my time I saw the visions of things to come, but I failed to see this child. I know now there was a reason for this. My people could grow and flourish, but they must first be a child; this is where it all begins, again and again.

Many people are One of each thousand, but there is only a single One of the One; He who carries the seed. He, the One through whom all wisdom is passed, and He who retains only that which is not evident, even to a child.

I remember being a child and yearning for the day when I would be a great warrior and hunter for my people. I would be the greatest hunter and provider that my people ever knew; I would create the legends. The day came, without my knowledge of its occurrence, that I saw the white buffalo, the symbol of who the Mother Earth really was. I came to know later that I would be the visionary of my people, the medicine man, he who possessed all the answers. I knew nothing! Until the day I passed into who I have become, I knew nothing. I helped my people through knowledge. Now, when it is too late, I wish I could return to help my people through wisdom.

This child cares where it matters, on the inside, through the heart, soul, and mind. Strangely enough, this child has no ability that all of the children of Mother Earth do not possess themselves. Was he struck with the likes of a big stick and commanded to awaken? Was he bestowed with a magical dream? Or was he selected from the time when innocence was most prevalent in his own mind? Only he can make that decision and he has yet to do so.

So tough on the outside is he, none can bend the branches of the mighty oak. Is he so tough? He sheds a tear for mankind! He caresses the flower in spring, touches the branch of a tree in awe, sympathizes with the stranger. He thirsts for knowledge and hungers for wisdom. When these things are given to him, he crumbles in their presence, believing himself not worthy. He is worthy, as are all the children of Mother Earth.

He will break the rules to benefit others but not himself. The hand will reach out in an effort to help, and he will scoff at those in self-imposed power and authority who bid him be silent. Those who say, "Let the people suffer that we may be revered. How dare he tell us we are equal? How dare he challenge our superiority, just who does he think he is?"

I tell you these things that you may come to know this child, that you may understand he is none that you are not. I tell you that you might understand these words are more than written words, they are more than knowledge, they are truly wisdom, and I have seen it.

So tough is this child that just at the time he has closed out all remaining sorrow, all remaining emotion, all remaining hatred, just at the time when he has preserved himself in the manner he deemed fit, he was awakened, touched, and his inner self was shattered beyond reproach, that he might not dare to try to change what would happen and he would receive without remorse that which will happen and question it.

Whether you think so or not, whether the child thinks so or not, and whether those who believe themselves superior think so or not, I challenged myself to answer that question, "Who does he think he is?" Again, whether anyone thinks so or not, he is—the Wolf. . . .

Author's Note

Chief Two-Pines's physical existence ended in 1869. This introduction appeared, unsolicited, in the final draft of the manuscript. Where it came from or how it came to be part of the manuscript I don't know. Like much of what is contained in this book, I am unfamiliar with its origin; but though I continue to question it, I accept it and ask that you accept it also.

Preface

I remembered, but not until the saga contained in these pages began to unfold, playing in the woods not far from my home. I was about nine years old I believe and, as most children are, very impressionable.

While playing in the woods with some friends (we weren't supposed to be there), I went off on my own near the river that ran through the woods. I stopped to skip a few rocks, something I was very good at for a young child. The river was not very wide where I stood and I challenged myself to skip the rocks upstream.

I had bent down to pick up some especially flat river rocks that I had spotted when I heard a light splashing sound and saw a reflection in the water. I looked up towards the sound and on the other side of the river I saw a beautiful white dog drinking from the river. He was a big dog and didn't seem to notice my presence.

I watched him drink for a moment and when he looked up at me I stood still, staring at his gaze. He seemed like a photograph as he stood there staring back at me. He lowered his head as if to drink again, but more like a bow. Then he turned slightly and I saw that he had been hurt, as he was covered in blood on his right side. I wondered if he had been shot or maybe kicked by a horse or a deer. He didn't seem to be in any pain and seemed not to notice that the wound was there. I remember that the wound was awful; it seemed to stretch from one end of his body to the other. I thought of walking across the river, as it wasn't very deep, to see if I could help, but knew all too well of the dangers of approaching an injured animal.

I looked around to see if any of my friends were nearby. I knew the dog needed help, but at that moment I was alone. When I looked back toward the dog, he was gone. I looked quickly around to see where he had run to, but he was not to be seen. I was sure he had run off and would die somewhere.

What I surely did not know then was that this animal was no dog, this animal was a wolf, a beautiful white wolf, and he had been injured badly.

I went back to skipping rocks until my friends came back. I thought no more of this encounter because, as children do, I once again got caught up in my play with my friends. The vision of the wolf had erased itself from my memory. But did it?

These pages contain the story of my brief encounter with an Indian Medicine Man named Standing Wolf. The details set forth his contacting me, his educating me, and his purpose in doing so. Standing Wolf would set me upon a path of learning unlike any other I have ever undertaken.

The challenge in the purpose of his contact was not clear at first, but as my tasks began to unfold, I was led to question my sanity, my intelligence, and my purpose of existence.

I had always thought I was ordinary, to a fault, with a flash of the extraordinary tossed in here and there. But the conflicts that arose in myself in a few short months and the learning of my purpose nearly pushed me over the proverbial edge. Perhaps the most detrimental realization was to learn that I would meet and challenge my own Phoenix.

I AM THE WOLF

I Am Awakened

March 11, 1991

When I awoke this morning, the alarm wasn't necessary; I had beaten it by nearly two hours. It had been an eventful sleep filled with dreams. I have been known to have some pretty fantastic dreams, but the dream of the previous evening was nothing less than cold. I thought nothing more of it as I forced myself up the stairs for my morning coffee and a dose of local news. Sunday was not a very newsy day around here, so my Monday morning paper was a fifteen-minute, less-than-stimulating jaunt.

It was a normal day at work, as far as you can stretch the meaning of the word *normal*. After a restless night's sleep, I was somewhat surprised that I wasn't tired; rather I was full of energy and eager to complete my tasks. My Monday night, however, gave me some cause for alarm.

I went to bed at around 11:00 P.M. and drifted off to sleep quickly; I was obviously more tired than I thought.

My same dream from the night before returned. I have had recurring dreams in the past; mostly I have had the same dream two or three times, always a little different but usually several months apart. I have never had the same dream two nights in a row, and it did not stop with two nights. This same dream that I had two nights in a row returned again and again, until I had the same dream, never changing, six nights in a row. When the dream repeated itself for the last time, I started to realize a few things the dreams were trying to tell me.

1

March 15, 1991

Sitting and staring into a campfire filled with snapping sounds and embers that floated into the night sky. Off in the distance I could hear howling wolves as they called to one another; they sounded in pain, but I did not know about such things. The closest I had ever been to a wolf was in a zoo, I am sure, save for the incident when I was nine years old; but I had forgotten that and still at this point had not recalled the incident.

As I sat and stared at the fire, I heard a crackling in the brush nearby. I looked toward the sound and saw, shining at me from the glow of the campfire, a pair of eyes, or what looked like a pair of eyes. Then it emerged from the brush and walked toward the fire and me, slowly. It was a beautiful creature, docile in its movements and very aware of my presence. It did not seem to be alarmed or afraid of me in any way. The animal continued toward me until it reached the fire, and I could see its entire presence. It was a beautiful creature, a perfect, healthy specimen that stood shoulder high to me when sitting. It was a wolf, a snowy, pure white wolf with the deepest blue eyes, which reflected like a mirror; I could see myself in them.

Without warning the wolf jerked his head to the sky and howled a deep howl. As I watched him howling, and thought how sad the sound was, I began to rise off the ground toward the sky, literally floating away.

Looking downward I could see the fire, myself, and the wolf. I looked up at the night sky filled with stars; it was a spectacular sight and I felt as if I could reach out and touch the stars one by one.

As I felt that I had stopped ascending, I heard a voice speak to me. I did not see anyone in my immediate presence; the voice had no traceable point of origin. I was amazed that this was happening to me and that I felt it happen and accepted it as normal. When the voice spoke, I believed it was an old voice as its gravelly sounds seemed to struggle to speak the words.

"See all there is here to see and wish to see it no more for it is the end of your physical existence."

I looked around for several moments; then next to me, among the stars, was a very old Indian man, who appeared out of nowhere. His face was worn and wrinkled. He looked hundreds of years old. His salt and pepper grey hair was as long as he was tall. He had a lone, dark blue feather suspended on the left side of his head; I could not see how it was attached. His eyes were black, almost as if he had no eyes at all. He was dressed in a black, flowing robe that either hung so low I could not see his feet; or he just didn't have any feet but in this place neither of us seemed to have a need for them, hanging in space.

"Who are you," I stated more than asked, still trying to sound as polite as I could. I looked down at the Earth, which seemed close enough to touch but definitely far away. I could see red blotches almost like fires burning all over the planet. It was eerie. The glowing fires would intensify, then dissipate, as yet others appeared and did the same.

"I am the mirror that reflects man's soul," he answered, if you can call that an answer.

"How profound," I replied, thinking that this was a dream and nothing really should make sense anyway. The Indian was motionless except for his flowing robe. I did not understand why the robe flowed as it did, I felt no breeze, I felt only the stillness of space.

"Life as you knew it lies ahead," the Indian spoke again. His voice was noticeably stronger, and he motioned with his arm as if inviting me into a room.

"I wonder what's going on down there?" I motioned toward the Earth, speaking of the fires.

"Phoenix is rising," the Indian said.

"Who?" I asked. Without an answer we began moving farther away from Earth, slowly at first, then with great speed. Past planets of the solar system, circling each as we traveled farther. He identified each planet we passed, but not with the names I knew them by and not with names I remember. He likewise named each nebula we encountered. I guess I wasn't paying attention because nothing he said soaked in. I just stayed in amazement at this thrilling dream. My attention span had temporarily escaped me, and I didn't seem to care; Earth was no longer in sight.

"Why are you showing me this?" I asked, truly expecting an answer. "Where are we going?" This was stuff astronauts dreamed of, not average people; although I do think of it once in a while.

"So that you may witness the result of your failure to change," he responded in a preaching tone. This dream was getting a little too bizarre, even for me.

As we continued to journey through space I saw a blinding white nebula and within it were what appeared to be four planets or meteors or something; they were like huge black rocks suspended within it. The nebula appeared to expand and contract like a great balloon. It swirled outward, then inward. I could have stayed out there in space forever, but this was a dream, right?

"This must be healed before you begin your journey," the Indian said. "It is at its time of beginning so the healing may be quick."

"What is your name? Heal what? Who are you?" I asked the Indian. He was still motionless. There was no response. "A name . . . do you have a name?" I asked again, this time more insistently.

"I am known by many names," came the reply. "To you I have but one. I am the prisoner of the beast within, he who longs to be free, to teach, and to release the pain of a thousand lifetimes. I am Standing Wolf."

As he had answered my question, within an instant I found myself seated at the campfire once again. I didn't even recall returning from wherever I was.

The campfire seemed different, its flames now danced in red and orange, instead of the bluish white I remembered them as before. Lying next to the fire was the white wolf I had left, only he was red, stained with blood, dead. His once blue eyes were gone, leaving black emptiness in their place. I reached out to touch the animal, but my hand did not connect.

I shot up in my bed and looked around my darkened room, wide-eyed. I was bathed in sweat. I shook my head and swung my feet over to the floor. "Still a great dream," I said sluggishly, rubbing my face and eyes. It was more like a television rerun, since that was the sixth time I had had the dream. At that point I was wondering when the dream would stop recurring. I had an old dream interpretation book and had attempted to look up everything I could think of in my repeating dream but could not find anything relating to my dream's events.

I stood and went into the bathroom. I turned on the light and looked at myself in the mirror; I looked like hell. I drew myself a glass of water from the faucet and drank it down eagerly, then drew another and returned to bed. I looked at the digital clock for the time, but it wasn't right; the clock showed 19:97 A.M. I reached over and slapped the clock a couple of times, and the time appeared, 4:31 A.M.

I crawled back into bed and remained motionless, but I did not fall back to sleep. I finally got up at 5:15 A.M. and headed for my morning coffee and newspaper. I would rather have slept in on a Saturday morning, but although I felt tired, I could not sleep.

As I sipped hot coffee and read my newspaper, flashes of my dream kept interrupting. I kept seeing the expanding and

5

contracting nebula, and I felt that it had some significance, since it was the last place visited in the dream. I had no idea what the significance could be, but if the dream came again, I would program myself to ask more specific questions, if that could be done.

Thought Speaks

For those of you who are unfamiliar with what automatic writing is, I can only explain it by telling you what it means to me. Automatic writing is the involuntary writing of facts and information that are received through the conscious memory, the spirit, or past experiences.

I have had many experiences with automatic writing but, keep in mind, I did not know what it was in the beginning. At first I did not understand the experiences, but as I began to absorb the information in the writings, I realized how wonderful their messages were. There was no way I could ignore them.

To many the messages will not be clear, so I offer my explanation of each writing. The true message is what each reader thinks it is. Whether the reader comes up with an explanation similar to or totally different from my explanation, no one can say it is wrong. As long as the message received provokes thought, depth of feeling, and a realization of how simple the Grand Creation and all that it entails is, then the message did get through and did invoke meaning.

The idea behind this book is to provoke thought in the mind of the reader. You will find that this book in no way will tell you how to live your life or carry on your daily activities, nor will it make any recommendations for changes you should make in your life. The whole idea is to make you stop and rationally think about who you are, what you are, and why you are here, the three big issues in life.

When the writings began it was as if I had no control of what was being written, and in essence I didn't. My hand was writing in the notebook, but it wasn't me. I could turn away, light a cigarette, close my eyes, or whatever, and the writing still came; it was like someone or something else had control of my hand. I only needed to think of a question sometimes, other times I just sat and the words came. I could never really comprehend what was being written. The next morning I would sit and read each word carefully and make an educated guess at its meaning. I would call Charmaine and read the words to her over the phone. Together we would come up with a myriad of explanations but rarely did we hit the mark. Just the same, discussing it gave much comfort to me.

The detailed writings began on July 3, 1991 and continued for several days. We could only awe at their content. Mostly the amazement was due to the simple beauty of what was said, and even if the explanations we thought of were wrong, they were just as beautiful. I later learned that they weren't wrong.

Each reader will have his or her own explanation of the meaning of each writing, and as long as the meanings make sense to each person, then they are correct. In other words, it doesn't matter what I think was meant by the writing—though I will tell you—it only matters what you think was meant.

July 3, 1991:

Mother Earth is the next of the first born, having once been a part of the One, then a family of two. When the Phoenix struck and broke her spirit, that which remained became the living Earth, with purpose. Her dying offspring, which remains attached to her to this date through an invisible umbilical cord, still affects its Mother as it screams its loneliness in the winds, the rains, and the tides. This child is Moon and will soon give of its physical existence in order to protect its Mother from the tragic remains of a dying universe not of its own. The dying child will weep upon its Mother and scar her deeply. The Wolf will witness the wounds and the healing will be seven hundred generations of physical life. Mother Earth will heal her own wounds but will first eradicate all interferences.

One can only guess at what this writing means, but my interpretation is simple. At one time the planet we call Moon was part of a single planet, as was the Earth and all of the planets and stars in our universe. It broke away from the one planet, perhaps through some catastrophe, and now orbits its closest Mother, Earth. It affects the weather: the rains, the winds, and the tides. I believe that each planet and each Mother Earth has such an affecting moon; they are all connected through the invisible umbilical cord to each other.

At some point a distant universe will be destroyed through some act of nature of its own, volcanic eruptions or perhaps a sun gone nova, and its fragments will rain down upon Earth. At some point larger fragments capable of doing much damage to Mother Earth will be blocked by—and will destroy—the Moon, sending its fragments to Earth. Damage from the meteors will be horrendous. Wounds will be healed by Mother Earth, but she will first eradicate all interferences (i.e., the loss of civilization in the areas of the wounds).

Natural disasters are best left to the healing powers of Mother Earth herself; man should not interfere. Everything happens for a reason. My greatest concern is *where* the larger fragments will strike Mother Earth.

July 3, 1991:

Phoenix is not a child of Mother Earth, rather the unborn seed, a seed Mother Earth would not wish to abort. It is the reverse of the benefits of Mother Earth; it is uncreation. The stability of the Mother depends on how well she can contain that which would harm her or her children. Once containment is breached, there is no turning back. When Mother Earth rumbles she is sealing the escape of the seed that man has opened. Man places much pressure on her wounds, and as they fester she heals herself. Like the unborn child at the end of its cycle, Phoenix longs to breathe and to be nourished. Phoenix will fear One of each Thousand, and the One will possess the knowledge, the wisdom, and the power of Mother Earth necessary to defeat him. When the power seals the wound, Phoenix shakes his spurious finger and spews forth the death and devastation in limitation as a reminder to Mother Earth of that which it seeks to do in totality. Only in the total darkness of day can Phoenix raise its head to survey the kingdom he seeks, as its face is so ugly Mother Earth could not bear her children to see it. Only then can Mother Earth breathe her deep sigh of despair. Mother Earth will protect her children as any Mother would, but the scornful child is blind and continues the childish spat in its Mother's face. Listen to the sigh, heard only by the One of each Thousand; its gossamer wings beat louder than thunder, strike sharper than lightning, with the accuracy of the arrow against a great wind. Like the invisible cobweb, its wings will touch one and all and generate an energy from each, and only the One of each Thousand will cry the tears of a cleansing. Run, child; fear, child; cry, child; this foretelling is inevitable. The birth shall be breach and the birth shall topple the Mother off her southern feet to begin the causing of a great tilt and the Mother will cry a massive frozen tear for the loss of her children. It begins.

It appears that though each of us has a spiritual Phoenix to face in his or her lifetime, a feeling or deep-seeded fear within, the Phoenix that Mother Earth will soon face is a physical one. I believe that Mother Earth's Phoenix is mankind, her children.

Mother Earth has battled for countless centuries to keep her Phoenix under control, to protect her children from it, from themselves; her efforts only now begin to fail. Mother Earth's

Phoenix is the opposite of all that she is; it is the refusal of her children to realize what she is, what she represents, that she is their well-being, their existence, their very life.

Mother Earth is all creation. Her opposite is uncreation or the end of Mother Earth. This writing suggests the end of Mother Earth will happen at the hands of her children. Man is destroying Mother Earth and doesn't seem to care. Little by little, day by day, he spits in her eye and denies that Mother Earth has given him all that he has. Man takes everything for granted.

To breach the containment of all that would harm the children upon Mother Earth would be to unleash all of the nuclear and other wastes that are stored within her, underground. As occurs when one has eaten tainted food, eventually the stomach will throw it up. The nuclear wastes stored within Mother Earth are harmful; they are tainted food that is killing her. Unleashing such wastes would certainly mean the end of the children upon Mother Earth. Her rumbling, or earthquakes, are Mother Earth's method of trapping harmful elements which might have otherwise found an escape route, away from her children. Man explains these earthquakes as natural occurrences; man is wrong. These natural occurrences are warning signs that Mother Earth is about to die.

Man places much pressure upon the wounds of Mother Earth; her wounds being the fault lines, cracks and wrinkles of age, that exist all over her. California is the prime example in North America. A lot of civilization lives upon the fault lines, which in turn places pressure upon them. The eruption of these faults is imminent, as is the downfall of the children who dwell upon them.

Not just California but worldwide, man knows where the wrinkles are; yet he ignores them and builds massive buildings and other structures right on top of them. Man begins new civilizations on the wrinkles and gives promises of prosperity and continued life that could never be. These acts that are taking place for no other reason than monetary gain for a select few will be seen throughout these writings.

I learned of the One of each Thousand that Phoenix will fear much later in my experiences. Of all the people that exist on Mother Earth at the time of her demise, one of each thousand will transcend the plane and will survive to renew the planet once more. *When* is what I had yet to learn.

Since there is no death and we are all to return to this place at some time in the future (or to another place similar to this one), the One of each Thousand is living now. Will the One of each Thousand return to this place, to this Mother Earth, or some other like her to begin again? I now believe so. I have further learned that my soul, my spirit, all that I was, have become, and will become is the One of the One of each Thousand. And this scares the hell out of me, though it gives me a certain amount of pride.

For example, if there were only one hundred million people on Mother Earth at the time of her ending, only a scant one hundred thousand would return. Imagine, the entire Mother Earth to be inhabited by no more than one hundred thousand children.

When Mother Earth's Phoenix spews forth his death and devastation, in limitation, this means a volcano, or probably more than one. All of them unleashing their violence upon Mother Earth at the same time or one shortly after the other. At the time of this writing, volcanos have been erupting in Japan and in the Philippines and soon in the Aleutian Islands. The people were not prepared and will not be prepared for the devastation that follows. Man thinks he is omnipotent; Mother Earth shall show him he is not.

Mother Earth's Phoenix can raise its head only in the total darkness of day, meaning during an eclipse. The last total eclipse of the sun was on July 11, 1991. I faced Phoenix on this date; I faced *my* Phoenix high in the mountains of Ecuador. He was beast without face but with tremendous powers. He had control over me in a way that I thought *no one* had. I was in charge of my life; I was in charge of my destiny, but my Phoenix had other ideas. I was being educated and my Phoenix, the fear within, did not like it.

Just what is the Phoenix? I have learned that there is nothing so great about the Phoenix; this is for sure. The Phoenix is self-doubt, self-pity, the lack of self-confidence. Each person has his or her own Phoenix and each person's Phoenix represents each person's greatest fears.

Mother Earth continually sends signals to her children that things are not right with her; but the children don't listen. Earthquakes are her shaking to try to alert us to the destruction we are doing to her. She tries to topple the buildings and other structures with her earthquakes that man has built over her wrinkles, her wounds, but man continues to rebuild, continuing his childish spat in her face. Man thinks he is superior and no one, not even Mother Earth, is going to tear down what temples he builds for himself.

The breach birth denotes massive destruction either by a volcano, earthquake, or both, in the southern hemisphere, mainly South America. The devastation will be so great that it will cause a shifting in the Earth's rotation, which could cause those lands that were once tropical to become glacial . . . the crying of a massive frozen tear. If this happens in the southern hemisphere—and I dread to tell you that it will, as I have seen it—what are we to believe will happen to the rest of the world? In my opinion, though it may be nothing good, it's about time.

Look at the mountains and ask yourself how they got there. Man has an explanation, but is it right? They are a shield against something. Are they a shield for the benefit of Mother Earth, or are they Mother Earth's shield for the benefit of her children, or are they a shield for Mother Earth to protect herself from her children? Perhaps they are a shield against ocean waters that will eventually flow at their feet.

What about those areas that children of Mother Earth cannot trespass; what is the reason for this? Just like man has no business in the center of Earth, and just like man has no business planting his poison beneath Mother Earth, there are certain areas on top of Mother Earth that man has no business transcending as well.

This writing causes me to ask several questions and I could go on forever, but I am sure you are thinking of your own questions. As you will find, that is the proper message: accept nothing; question everything. Your very existence could depend upon your ability to question what you see, accept it as real, and put it to use toward your very existence.

July 3, 1991:

The plague of Phoenix upon Mother Earth's most sensitive children is a picking. The poisonous talons have already begun the snatching of the lives from the heated south, the feet, to the misty northwest, the head. Her children are made to bleed at the heart of the wounds, and their blood is the stench of death to their own. These children despair and Mother Earth mourns the loss of her greatest achievements, men who love men, women who love women, and the ability to bear no ill will toward each other or anyone. The perfect society falls, and Mother Earth grasps at the great emptiness at her bosom. When mankind and womankind possess the ability of an unrelentless love of all, the pains it causes the Phoenix infuriates him, and the unsex is the delivering of a mournful blow to Mother Earth. The battle is on and Mother Earth will soon call upon the One of each Thousand to take up her shield. Make them ready, make them strong, make them know. Damned will be those who show these children compassion; the plague will strike at them too. The heart aches for the loss of the unrelentless love, lest it

14

take leave forever and Mother Earth will throw down her will to survive and the masses will suffer as those most sensitive. Heal them; I will show you the way. The Moray Eel must die. The Phoenix spews forth his own cure and the farmers of the plains produce the remedy. Mother Earth gives of herself that her children shall have all they require; see it, see it; it is there. Of the One of each Thousand, only the one who will lead the ones of each thousand will see it clearly. She cries, cries, harder she cries; save my child; let him die no longer. Seek his hospice in the alfalfa fields. Restore to Mother Earth her most sensitive children, and the pride in the saving will drive Phoenix deeper into its grave. The One of the One of each Thousand must spirit; the fields not to be graves. The Cotopaxi calls to him. Seek him now, the answer to be found at the Cotopaxi; and her name is Reeva. Listen; learn; save my child from the illness upon them.

Obviously Standing Wolf was aware of my having to deal with the AIDS virus personally. I am not afflicted, but I have lost friends and acquaintances to the disease and at the time he contacted me, two additional friends, one male and one female, were both struggling with the disease. Having this problem heavy on my mind, he felt it necessary to offer these words in order to clear my mind for what lay ahead, but I did not listen.

The snatching of lives in the heated south refers to Africa and the southern continents. The misty northwest means northern California, San Francisco. The heart of her wounds are fault lines and children who bleed, and their blood is the stench of their own death, meaning AIDS. San Francisco has the largest gay population in North America; Minneapolis/St. Paul is the second largest (and is not on a fault line).

The mournful blow, the unsex, is Phoenix's way of destroying the children of Mother Earth in an area where they cannot easily repopulate. The Phoenix is mankind itself and the destruction is AIDS, a man-made disease. Damn those who try to assist these AIDS-stricken children, the medical profession, and the families of the afflicted, for Phoenix will strike at them, too. Should Mother Earth throw down her protective shields—the ability instilled in her children to ward off disease—the immune system, then everyone will suffer just as those who are now afflicted with AIDS.

I have been unable to figure out the meaning of the Moray Eel in this passage, other than that to most Native Americans it is a negative sign of those who try to impress their will upon others, such as in organized religion, governments, or the military.

The Phoenix, mankind, spews forth his own cure, the cure being found on the fruited plains. So the children of Mother Earth die no longer from this disease and seek his hospice in the alfalfa fields. Alfalfa is a natural blood purifier. There is a recipe found elsewhere in this book for its use. This natural blood purifier is not mentioned to encourage AIDS-afflicted readers to cease their current medical treatment in exchange for alfalfa teas. Curing this disease will send Phoenix deeper into its grave. As will be addressed in other areas of this book, AIDS is a man-made disease; it was initially intended for chemical warfare.

The Cotopaxi, which calls to Phoenix, is a mountain high in the Andes of Ecuador. There, Phoenix was met and challenged. Reeva played several roles in a scant forty-eight-hour period. She was the source of much wisdom that I had not yet obtained by the time of the challenge.

July 4, 1991:

Since development, the structure of mankind has remained unchanged. Only woman is of the Earth, man of the woman. Mother Earth keeps her children lean with purpose. The development over the wounds causes great stress and much building over the wounds which she is desperate to heal. Her methods are as orthodox as the sun. When man lies down with man and woman lies down with woman, the development over the wound is stagnate and the great pressures are relieved. When the burden becomes too great, she shakes to topple the weight to allow for further healing. Her failure to warn her own children, her most perfect children, is a lie. When the turning inside out of the great northwest city occurs, loss of life will be tremendous. The warnings have been sent; the spatting continues. The One of the One of each Thousand will soothe her ravaged breast. Greed, avarice, and ignorance from Earth Mother to Earth child; the child refusing to acknowledge, share, continue. Stretch out the mighty hand of the One of the One in compassion. Care for the child who is seed, who is infant, who is boy, who is man; bid them heed the warning of the third day of the third month, a number of year is unimportant. This is the one day of each year when Mother Earth breathes. Soon the sickness man buries within her will cause the breath to end in a cough, and the civilization surrounding the wound will fall and rise no more. Only the perfect childs will endure. You have held my hand in the Valley of the Sun. I have touched your essence in the temple of healing. Hold in your knowing that I am not for the One, but the many. Extend your great knowledge; smile your great smile; they will hear you. Let them not reach out to you, for you are not prepared. Man does not believe in the young. I will change you, feed you, and believe in you for them. Pity the foolish; they need you most. Scorn the ignorant; they deserve her wrath. Mine was once a compassionate existence; I have since learned to hate, for only after we have learned to hate will we understand love and learn of its awesome power. The time for hate has come to its plateau. The word of self love, love given, love shared is nigh. I task you; take my challenge. I held hate for you once, but the alternative is evident. I am here for you, and the love I give to

17

you is the greatest you have yet to accept. See me; hear me; I am the host of your original soul.

This writing suggests there are too many people living in the areas of the wounds, which I have determined are fault lines in Mother Earth. Keeping her children lean (barren) with purpose, means keeping them from reproducing and placing more pressure on the wounds.

When the burden becomes too great she shakes (earthquakes) to topple the weight to allow for further healing; the weight being buildings and other heavy objects.

The turning inside out of the great northwest city (San Francisco area) and the tremendous loss of life means everyone who lives there will die.

The warnings that have been sent can only mean the previous earthquakes and previous rumblings that have gone on over the years. This would be all the warning I need.

Greed, avarice, and ignorance can only indicate that the warnings have not been listened to; and in order to further monetary gain, man continues to build and put pressure on the wounds.

The third day of the third month, March 3, is supposedly when "it" will happen. I don't like the statement that a number of year is unimportant; this isn't much of a warning, but is it? Does this mean that it is going to happen soon or that it won't happen in my physical lifetime, so why worry?

The sickness man buries within her can only be nuclear waste that is buried underground around the world. I have always thought that stashing this garbage beneath the Earth was a big mistake. We are led to believe that it is safe to store this mess underground, but then, our own government is telling us this, so I have to doubt it. Past history has told us that our own government will withhold the truth from its own citizens at the drop of a hat.

The rest is pretty easy to figure out. *I am the host of your original soul* tells me that I am the incarnate for Standing Wolf.

July 5, 1991:

The value of an individual life is that which it reaps within itself and not in the face of others. Mother Earth sees no monetary value in her children. All that is hers is theirs to share equally—that which man reaps from her surface or plants beneath it. That which lies below her surface is in its grave and will emerge in its own due time. All riches lie in knowledge and no other place. The heart is the keeper of each man's self-worth. That which is the keeper is capable of generosity in giving. Man created monies to keep himself in reverence over his fellow man. Amass no more than sustenance requires for to do so is weakness. He who appears worthless on the outside possesses a heart of gold. His goodness is the enemy of Phoenix, who is monetary.

This writing was easy for me. The explanation is short and so simple that it makes me ask questions of my own. Why are we so self-conscious about what others may think of us? Is it not so that we were given a gift of life and that we are truly worth all that such a gift entails? If you can answer such a question then perhaps we are.

We are worth what we think we are worth and nothing else. It's what is inside that counts and no matter how much others try to discount what we think of ourselves, they won't be around after this world is gone, so pay them no mind.

July 5, 1991:

Choose thy champion carefully, for he will strike you down in countless ways before your inner purpose emerges to defeat him. You are One of the One of each Thousand—he knows this; though he will not recognize you, he fears you. Use his fear wisely, for your victory must be your own; I can offer no help. As you question me, I will challenge you further to answer yourself. My hand forever on your shoulder, my heart forever leading your team. That which you seek lies in my defeat, but I am not your champion, I am your equal. Accept all that is and question all that is not. Look back and draw on your tribulations for guidance, for you can never fail yourself. Mother Earth accepts all who accept themselves and her. She demands nothing of you but expects much. You are your own champion.

The One of each Thousand represents those who will return after the end of Mother Earth, perhaps after a million years of healing; the date and time are uncertain. Being the One of the One of each Thousand is perplexing. I have debated with Charmaine about this at length, and the only solution we can come up with is that One will be the chief, One will lead the others, and Standing Wolf is the One. Being the incarnate of Standing Wolf must mean that I am also the One—a scary thought.

Choosing a champion, one who will lead each of us from within, means choosing ourselves. We are our own champions and have the final say, the final determination as to the life we lead and where that life will lead us.

Inner fears must be conquered and we all fear something, which is our inner fear. In order for us to progress, grow, and live the way Mother Earth intended, we must conquer our inner fears. I came to learn later that the inner fear in each of us represents our Phoenix. People's fears are driving them crazy, so to speak, and making them do unspeakable things. They are going against each other and the inner fears (fear of oneself) are the cause. People do not handle stress well; we snap at a moment's notice. We are quick to judge others in order to save ourselves from being judged. When you hear the term *Phoenix rising* I believe it means people are at or near the end of their ropes.

You are your own champion. Only you can overcome your inner fear, your Phoenix, and no one can help you better than you can help yourself. I believe that if we all look inside ourselves for that bit of hope, no matter how small, as long as we can find some, take hold of it, and put it forward in our lives, then we as a people, worldwide, can come together. When you grasp the hand of a stranger upon first meeting or introduction and you say how pleased you are to meet them, do you mean it? I have yet to find anyone who really means it, sad to say—even myself.

July 5, 1991:
   You ask the extraordinary; seek me not for this purpose.
   Your mind works well, as it should. Seek yourself and know that you are not ready.

I do not know what this writing means. However, I include it here in case you do. Obviously I was thinking of a question or something, or perhaps just seeking an answer. If anyone has an opinion as to its meaning, please drop me a note.

July 5, 1991:
   I speak in many tongues; your hand reads like the prophet; you are not prophet; the One of the One is a greater truth. I speak not to your ears, but mind. The mind will comprehend what the eyes will not and absorb what the ears refuse. You are the seed, the infant, the boy, the man. Revere them all as they will reveal the truth of your heart's desires and your mind's wanderings, and be the nourishment of your soul.

This tells me why I could not hear Standing Wolf but could understand him. Don't believe everything you see and hear.

21

You are the seed: the stages of life from infant to boy to man. Live through the lessons learned. Let your heart and your mind wander; it is good for the soul. I guess if we are happy with ourselves, if we love ourselves, we are nourishing ourselves and this provides the opportunity to share inner goodness with others. Let's face it, if we are not happy with ourselves, if we do not love ourselves, how can we feel and share such things with others? Not being happy with ourselves can make us mighty bitchy to everyone else. There was a time when I thought I had the market cornered on bitchy; maybe you've felt the same way. As I go through life and encounter those who are not happy in life or happy with themselves, I have learned that there is a lot of room in that corner.

July 5, 1991:

You will not teach, but you will be called upon to share. When the words are not there, I will provide them. Speak with whomever you wish; it is encouraged. Bid them speak further as the plateau slopes still.

I must have been asking the purpose of the writings I was receiving and what I was to do with them. Being called upon to share, I am convinced, means making this book happen.

When the words are not there . . . You just wouldn't believe how the words came when I could not find them while compiling this book. They actually appeared in my computer overnight. In any area where I struggled to find the words, they came and they were not mine. I confess that my co-author is Standing Wolf and I credit him with much help, which I often needed. I am not a writer by trade and his help has been truly beneficial.

I was further encouraged to speak with others regarding what was happening, the writings, the journeys, and so on. It helped me greatly to get through what you will eventually agree were trying times.

July 5, 1991:
    Your concern for this virus is noble and gracious. Its time has come; if you tell them, they will listen. Be accepting of your grief, for it shall become surmountous. I grieve with you. Grief is but the hardening of the soul, it will escape you never. Sing the praises for the spiritual self of those who pass as it rises on to its next achievement. The memory is the presence of those moved on. They will speak to you there. Your compassion is thrilling to a tear. This is a necessary benefit. Mother Earth accepts each with an open heart. She returns them in countless ways. Beware, Phoenix will strike at you when you are weak. Strike back with health, strength of conviction, and knowledge of purpose. Shake hands with the virus that concerns you and strike it with your tears. Embrace the children of the bloody disease, give to them the love they have lost and let your mind be at ease with the coming grief. That which does not kill us makes us stronger; that which does kill us has found a weakness. Phoenix thrives on weakness. Take him by his grasp and throw him to the Wolf. Haunt me no more with this issue. I have provided all that you seek. This illness is a given.

    I was either at a point where I was still unsure about what Standing Wolf had tried to tell me about the AIDS virus or I was still upset about the entire disease as I had been visiting with a friend who is HIV positive. Many people do not give the disease a second thought, even some of those who have it. I, however, found that I was preoccupied with it.
    Telling me that my grief will become surmountous leads me to believe that many will die from this disease before anything is done or a cure is found.
    Those who die from this disease or for any other reason

will rise on to their next achievement, their next life, if you will. You need a concept of reincarnation to follow this. Even those who die will continue in our memory; this is true.

Phoenix will strike when you are weak, when your defenses are down, even in a time of sorrow. I have known many people to do things out of sorrow or sympathy that they would not otherwise do. Staying healthy, having strength in the knowledge that your life has meaning—these things keep you on top, give you purpose, which is what we all seek.

That which kills us has found a weakness. This is why staying healthy and knowing you have purpose are so important. Not possessing these things within is the weakness.

Take him by his grasp and throw him to the Wolf. We all have a "wolf," our inner strength within—this is all that's necessary to defeat the Phoenix.

July 5, 1991:
Time is but a rising and setting of the sun; it only has purpose if you allow it. Time can be precious; do not give of it to learn that which you have known all along.

Do not waste time chasing after dreams or answers that you have known all along. If you seek validation, you need look no further than your inner self.

This is a simple description of the writing, but I still question why in one statement I was told that time only has purpose if I allow it, then in the next that time can be precious. I won't dwell on my own question, I haven't the time.

July 5, 1991:
Incarnate, as you were, as you are, as you will be.

I must have been consciously questioning what an incar-

24

nate is and this is the answer I was given. I believe that we are our own incarnate in many forms.

July 5, 1991:
You possess this; find it and give of it freely.

As with a previous writing, I cannot explain what this writing means, but I include it in case you can. I must have been seeking something. Again, if anyone has an idea about its meaning, please drop me a note.

July 6, 1991:
The soul, unlike the spirit, is not immortal—except to Phoenix. It can cease for a blink of an eye or for the passing of generations. Yours is the soul of the eye that does not blink and the generations that do not pass but continue. You have challenged my authority and have questioned my presence, never an answer demanded. I thought you not foolish, I thought you curious. The story teller will seek to make the presentment. You will not know him; he will know you and call you in utterance, "You are the Wolf?" You will know him to be the seeker, the tool, the story teller. Begin the journey of words that you should be prepared; the year of the One, the Nines and the Seven grows near. Know his hair, for it is dark; know his eyes, for they will shine with the thirst for truth; know his mouth, for it will speak in innocence; know his body, lean; and know his hands, they be cold. His is the apprentice who will be your story teller. Seek the deep of his mind and instill there that which is necessary for the presentment. Seek out the early arrival of your soul, spirit, child to be. Soul hardened, heart pure, mind thirsty. This will be as the great race; time for none other until the task is complete. Come to the mountain where the restless spirit awakens to cause you challenge. Prepare for the changing of the sentinel, it scoffs the champion.

At One and Nine hours, Nine minutes, Seven seconds, the breath will be drawn; the change occurs. Strike out with the eye of the Wolf and its hue of sky will blind the ugly beast. Let him see not all that he seeks to survey; let him breathe not the air of your chest. Bid him, "I have come and know that I am not alone"; the witnesses, blinded also. Touch their temple, that its memory be clear, and leave them at peace. The Wolf is kind; the Wolf is strong; the Wolf will die. Bleed not on the mark of the talon, for it gives cause for return. I am the Wolf; I am the Wolf; I am the Wolf; and my coat of color, of souls pure, darkens red with the stain of the spirits it releases. Mother Earth is weak and can not seal the wound. Stand upon its widening gape and speak my name; I will appear to you for the exchange. Child in darkness, man in light, I will take your hand and feel of its true purpose, and return you to your original place, where you shall see me no more. I mourn for this day, One of the One, Son of my Son; ignore the tear that falls. The change is the passing of the spirits, a time of much happiness.

The spirit can either be reborn immediately or it can take the passing of several generations before it is called upon again.

My spirit is a continuous one. I learned later on that even before my spirit no longer exists, another has been made ready to take its place and the spirit continues to pass from one to the next, here on this Mother Earth. This is a little disturbing because I met the One who will inherit my spirit. I thought him nothing like me, but then, I am nothing like Standing Wolf either, so I cannot judge.

I met him at Point Dume (Malibu) in California in August 1991. He was a rather nice fellow and he knew exactly who I was. I have had to refer to my sketchy notes, but I believe his name was Robert. He called to me, "You are the wolf?" and it was all I could do to keep my balance.

We had a nice conversation, but I can't remember a thing

we discussed. Perhaps I am not supposed to remember, but I do recall that he didn't appear to be in any hurry to inherit my spirit—thank whomever for that small favor! I still insist that he is not the story teller and argued with Charmaine just before publication of that fact. But we could be mistaken. This writing describes him exactly as he appeared.

Seek out the early arrival of your soul, spirit . . . As I mentioned, my spirit appears to be continuous and the One who will inherit it is now alive and living on this Mother Earth. If this Robert is the One who will inherit it, I hope he has a good sense of humor and I wish him luck. I have laid some ground rules in my lifetime that will be pretty hard to follow.

The changing of the sentinel, the one who watches over the Mother Earth, I believe, is Standing Wolf. The challenge I took saw me change places with him and fight a battle for Mother Earth in a way that he could not. Standing Wolf is spirit and I gave him body for the challenge.

One and Nine hours, Nine minutes, Seven seconds (1997, again!), the time the change between myself and Standing Wolf occurred, was also on July 11, 1991, and the exact time of the last total eclipse of the sun.

The eye of the Wolf was given to me by Reeva, the woman who played many parts in my experiences with Standing Wolf. Its purpose and use will be detailed later.

I never learned who the witnesses were/are. I did not meet or see anyone else before, during, or after the challenge, but I did feel their presence.

The explanation for the remainder of this writing is laid out in the section titled "Confrontation."

July 6, 1991:

She is of this Earth and my vision intact. You are of this Earth and all that I am. Erase this doubtful thought, for this is truth. There is death in doubt; there is love in truth.

This was a response to my questioning of the woman called "Reeva." I had asked whether or not she was alien. This response told me that Standing Wolf was blind or had been blinded by the challenger. Reeva provided his vision and I provided everything else he needed. I guess I was too blind to see what needed to be seen.

The details on the coming challenge were finally laid out. I was left with a lot of questions after this writing, but was told to question all that was not.

July 6, 1991:

The power lies in the eye for it is the hardened bone of its immortal soul. To return it to Phoenix is to return him to his time of beginning; he is unaware. It must be cast into the fog of blindness, that there be light for a thousand generations, that all may serve Mother Earth in her time of healing. Great despair will lie in the failure and the act will pass unnoticed. Like the White Wolf in snow, the trail of its past is seen, the uncertainty of its future known only to the One. Take certain caution in the challenge and emerge as the Wolf for one and ninety-seven days upon success. Victory attained by the One for the benefit of many. Yours will be the ignorance, the doubt, the skeptical, and innocence lost, forever and never to be found ordinary again. The time and place of the challenge has been set; you are expected. Beware, Phoenix has prepared for the meeting for a thousand years, that he might reign a thousand more. Know him by his voice that speaks to your mind. Its sounds will be pleasing and you will think it mine. Know that you have never heard my voice, as it was taken from me a thousand years ago. That which you have heard is the truth of the spirit, the truth of the soul, and the truth of love—strength in all three.

Turn and behold the Wolf, greet him and bid him be at

28

your side for the journey ahead. He is the keeper and the defender of your essence. Seek me no further until his coat is red. Call upon your memory for guidance; I have placed much of the unspoken there.

The largest part of this writing I will not explain because it too is detailed in the section titled "Chronicles." However, the paragraph that begins "Turn and behold the Wolf" was fascinating, as this was the first time I actually met the Wolf. As I sat at my desk in my house, I turned in my chair and there he was, a snowy white wolf. I was stunned by his appearance and his beauty. He had the deepest blue eyes I had ever seen. He sat motionless and just looked at me. When I turned in my chair for just a split second, he was gone. Perhaps a vision, perhaps not.

This was the last of the writings from Standing Wolf and as you can see, there was still much unexplained information regarding the challenge to come and many other things. *Call upon your memory for guidance; I have placed much of the unspoken there.* I always knew what to do in any situation on my journey because of the "unspoken" that had been placed in my memory.

Drawing made during automatic writing, July 6, 1991

Turn and behold the ones greet him and
bid him be at your side for the journey ahead,
he is the keeper and the defender of your essence,
seek me no further until his task is set.
Call upon your memory for guidance, I have
placed much of the unspoken there.

Drawing made during automatic writing, July 6, 1991

It Begins

I had made the decision in early July 1991 to journey to the Cotopaxi Mountain in South America, as beckoned by Standing Wolf. I determined that I should arrive in time for the total eclipse of the sun, which was to occur on July 11, 1991.

My flights seemed uneventful, as I had much on my mind—except for my Miami to Lima connection. I was befriended by a flight attendant named Reeva. I knew something was unusual about our meeting but decided to let it flow rather than question it.

Reeva was a very nice-looking woman, obviously of South American descent. She seemed to pay rather close attention to me, and when her on-board duties were done, she sat in the vacant seat next to mine. She made small talk, asking if I had business in South America. I knew all too well that she knew exactly why I was going to South America—or did she?

I decided to play the game and told Reeva that I was going to the Cotopaxi Mountain in Ecuador to photograph the eclipse. Reeva told me that the best view would be from the top, out of the trees. She wore an interesting necklace, a bluish-colored rock on a leather rope, which she removed and handed to me. She asked if I would throw it into the Cotopaxi volcano when I arrived; it would bring her luck, she said. I took the necklace and looked at it closely. Besides the unusual color, it had what appeared to be carved markings in it and if it was held just right, it looked like an eye. It had a small hole in one end that did not appear to be drilled—it was not a perfect hole—and that the leather string fed through. I placed the necklace in my carry-on bag and assured her that I would do as she asked.

When I arrived at Lima International Airport, I was met by a young local man who offered me a ride to my hotel. I accepted the offer, although I didn't know which hotel I would be staying at. I decided to let the man take me where he must have known I was to go. The driver left me at the Lima Sheraton. I checked in and went to my assigned room and immediately called Charmaine. I told her about Reeva, the necklace, and the young man who brought me to the hotel. I was already into my second rum and Coke (I always carry a small bar when I travel; one never knows).

I resolved to get some sleep and prepare for the next day's adventure. I was sure it would be an adventure because it had been one so far. Sleep was hard to find; visions of what to expect the next day kept popping into my head. A meeting and a challenge didn't sound all that hard, but this was to be my greatest challenge, I was told.

I awoke early. I didn't know the time, but looked out my window and since there wasn't much activity, I surmised it was fairly early. When I turned from the window, there at the foot of the bed was the Wolf. He sat motionless, staring at me. I acknowledged his presence by saying, "Hi there," or something like that, but I had learned that acknowledging him at all was fruitless. I went about preparing to leave for my journey, showering quickly and guzzling coffee brought by room service. I didn't remember ordering coffee and I had no appetite, so I did not eat the rolls that came with it. All the while the Wolf remained at the foot of the bed. The young man who brought the coffee did not seem to notice him, which was strange. I would think if one walked into a hotel room and saw a pure white wolf, that such a person would have something to say, but nothing. After dressing, I grabbed my camera bag and

33

headed out of the hotel to catch a taxi. Somehow I knew I was going to an airfield, I just knew.

During the entire taxi ride I had this knotted feeling in my stomach. I had the feeling that I should have stuck with my first instincts and stayed home. It was a little too late to change my mind now; the best thing to do was stick it out and get it over with.

The Wolf kept staring at me, motionless, as if he was trying to instill some kind of answer, some kind of power in me. My confidence was not as high as it could have been but the Wolf seemed to help. I had no idea what was going to happen, but according to that feeling in the pit of my stomach, it was either going to be something devastating or something wonderful. I had to somehow rid myself of the uncertainty I was feeling. Then and only then would I be able to understand the outcome of whatever would happen, or be able to enjoy it—whichever the case would be. Either way, according to my notes, whatever was going to happen that day was not far off. I began to hum lightly to calm myself. I had not eaten that day, but I felt as if I could throw up. The Wolf let out a low whine as if he were in pain. I made eye contact with him and his blue eyes sparkled, almost like the flashbulb on a camera. God, I felt helpless.

Suddenly, I had a vision, a flash. It could not have lasted more than a split second but it seemed like forever. It was almost like watching it on a movie screen and what I was watching was not very pleasant. I was hovering high above a great city; I came to learn that the city was San Francisco. I hovered over houses, apartment buildings, and large office buildings in the downtown area. I could see a trolley car moving slowly along its route. People were everywhere, on the streets, in cars, and in boats in the bay.

Then, without warning, a great fissure opened in the Earth on the west end of the city. A great gust of air rushed out, causing the ground to begin rumbling. Then, the rumble became a powerful shaking and buildings began to topple. People in the streets ran helpless, seeking shelter. Another fissure opened not far from the first, then another, and another, until the entire ground below me looked like a dry, cracked desert.

The gusts of air continued, more buildings and more houses crumbled as the fissures grew wider and swallowed up their remains. In what appeared to be a great last effort, all that I could see appeared to blow up, but there was no fire, no real explosion. Then, as quickly as it happened, it was over. Nothing was before my eyes but water, a great expanse of water, and the city of San Francisco was gone.

I jerked in the back seat of the taxi cab, like one might when coming out of a daydream. I looked at the Wolf, who hung his head low and shut his eyes tight. I wondered if he had shown me a vision of what was yet to come and, if so, when. The Wolf let out his low whine once more as the taxi pulled up to the airfield where I was to meet the pilot of my uncertainty.

[I am not certain if this vision was a forewarning of something that will happen, but we all know how dangerously close San Francisco—all of California for that matter—is to devastation and destruction from earthquakes.]

I paid the driver, handsomely, judging from the resounding thanks I got, which were more than gratuitous. I still did not have the currency exchange down right; but what the hell, somehow I had already spent more than I had taken with me, although I never seemed to lack money.

The pilot was standing next to the helicopter, surveying the craft as pilots do prior to a flight. I walked over and held out my hand to introduce myself. The pilot turned to face me; it was a woman.

"Names are not important," she said in perfect English. "Just pay me my fare and we will leave."

I did as she asked and handed over the money. She briefly

counted it and looked at me with that look I kept getting from people, who told me I didn't know how much money I was handing over.

"I really don't care," I said, preventing her from saying anything about the money. "Let's just get on with it."

We boarded the helicopter for our flight to the Cotopaxi in the Equadorian Andes. I took the copilot's seat, though I knew nothing about flying. If my pilot were to suddenly bail out or drop dead, I would certainly be at the mercy of a pending crash. My copilot, the Wolf, was behind my seat. At times I thought it was great that nobody other than I could see the animal; but at other times I thought it a shame that others were not able to behold this beautiful creature.

The Wolf panted and stared at the floor. It wasn't that hot in the early morning; it was as if he was psyching himself up. He kept staring at the floor, never moving or making a sound other than panting.

The helicopter began its ascent slowly, then veered off toward the mountains before it was more than fifty feet off the ground.

"You been flying long?" was my vain attempt at making conversation.

"Long enough to get you where you need to be," she answered. She looked at me out of the corner of her eye and did so several times during the flight.

We flew over towns and villages; they all looked so small, menial. I tried in vain to make out landmarks for whatever reason, but this was a strange area and I did not know where I was. We could not have been more than a thousand feet off the ground. I felt as though I could reach out and touch some of the buildings.

"Why do you want to go to the foot of the Cotopaxi?" she asked. "There's nothing there."

"I was hoping to get some good film of the eclipse today," I replied.

"But the sun will be blocked by the trees," she said.

"Well, I'll walk up the mountain until I reach a spot where I can see it clearly and set up my cameras there . . . "

"We're almost to the border," she interrupted. "And the Wolf, he is your guide?" she continued.

"Wolf?" I was mildly shocked.

"The one who follows you, the one behind your chair." She had a slight tremble in her voice.

"Ah, shit!" I shouted. "No questions, just fly this thing, okay?" There was silence for the remainder of the flight. How did this woman see the Wolf when no one else seemed to? Or was it that everyone else saw him as well and said nothing? I didn't even want to ask questions of myself. I thought I had stopped doing that several days ago and decided to let whatever happened happen.

The helicopter began to descend. The mountains were beautiful; a haze hung low over the trees. The helicopter landed and I proceeded to open the door.

"This *is* a one-way flight, right?" my pilot asked.

"So I am told," I replied. I got off the helicopter and tried to stay low, away from its blades.

She had landed it in a very tight clearing that seemed to just accommodate the aircraft. I looked behind my seat as I got off for the Wolf; he was gone. I looked around the area outside the helicopter to see if I could spot him, but he was nowhere. As I closed the door, the helicopter began to take off before I had a chance to get away from it. It was gone in seconds. I could hear its beating blades in the distance as it flew away—a lonely sound.

I stood and surveyed the area where I was left. It was desolate, not a soul around. I wondered about the "witnesses" that were supposed to be there. I began to walk away from the area, in no specific direction, just walking. I wanted to think I knew where I was going, but I didn't.

Confrontation

As I stood there on the side of the Cotopaxi Mountain, eye of the Wolf in hand, I felt as if a thousand eyes were upon me. I also had the distinct feeling that it was a little too late to turn back now. It is hard to describe what I was feeling and what was running through my mind at the time. I am usually a fairly confident person, but I still felt I was at the mercy of my feelings. All I could do was wait. I turned in circles as I looked around at the mountain; it was misty and the branches of the trees and bushes hung low.

A slow, chilling breeze began to waft over the area where I stood, which was strange since the sun was so hot. I strained to look up, as much as I dared myself to view the solar eclipse that had scarcely begun. I looked at my watch, but it had stopped at nine minutes past the hour of ten—I knew it was later than that now. The eclipse had not yet darkened the skies, but I could see the sun was being slowly eaten away by the shadow of the Moon. Clouds were all around, but a clearing over my head allowed the sun to shine through.

I heard a low grumble off in the distance, probably the sound of some animal nearby. It came again, but this time stronger and louder. I looked around for the best way to exit and I was ready to leave that very instant, but for some reason my feet would not move. The sky slowly grew dark from the shadow of the Moon. I looked around, quickly jerking my head from side to side. Those thousand eyes that I had felt previously were still watching. In an instant I found myself standing near the top of the mountain. I could feel its rumble and its move-

39

ment beneath my feet. I could only guess how I got there, but I had a pretty good idea. I looked around at the trees in the forest below. The solar eclipse was almost to corona; I could barely see. The chilling feeling I had felt earlier still had not gone away. I wished I had a coat.

Suddenly, with a slow rumble at first and slowly building stronger, the Earth began to shake beneath my feet.

"Who . . . are . . . you?" came a thunderous voice from out of nowhere.

I looked quickly around. "Trouser check," I said.

"Speak, ignorant one!" the voice came again in a commanding tone.

The Earth shook again. I found myself thinking aloud, "Okay, play time!"

"Who's there?" I asked the thin air.

"You do not come to question me," the voice replied. At that instant I heard the words of Standing Wolf return to my head, "I have come and know that I am not alone." I looked toward the misty Earth below me.

"I have come and know that I am not alone!" I yelled, my voice as strong as I could make it.

"So, One of the One," I heard the voice again, "you come to challenge me once more!" The Earth shook violently this time. A thick fog began to rise up below my feet. I felt sick; I wanted to puke. The ugly fog rose up thicker around my feet—brown, orange, and dirty yellow.

"I am the Wolf," I yelled.

"Then you shall soon be a dead wolf," the voice returned.

I had some news for him: I had been standing on that mountain since 7:30 that morning and I already felt like a dead man, wolf—whatever! I was chilled to the bone and soggy from my trek through the woods. I thought of a hot shower and the nice warm bed that waited for me at home, that is, if I ever saw home again—realization returned. I had no face to go with the voice that spoke to me; however, it was a voice that definitely meant business.

Once again the Earth shook, more violently than ever before. A crack in the surface of the Earth opened beneath me. I jumped back to avoid falling into the great ravine.

"Bring forth the Wolf!" the voice commanded in anger.

"I am the Wolf!" I cried. The sky above was completely blackened now from the eclipse. Only the corona of the sun was visible. I don't know if it was the ground that shook or my knees, but something caused a nauseating movement. I fell backwards away from the widening crack in the Earth's surface.

"Call forth the Wolf!" the voice commanded again as a burst of pure white energy shot out from the fog before me and struck me all over. I felt as if I had been struck by lightening.

"Call . . . forth . . . the . . . Wolf!" the voice commanded again, speaking each word slowly and in anger. Two more bursts of energy struck me from within the fog. I quickly rolled to the side to avoid them, but they followed me. I cried out in pain. The corona of the sun burned like a golden ring in the sky. The fog loomed before me, growing bigger, darker; and it appeared to be filled with anger, strength. I thought of how this kind of thing only happens in the movies. Standing Wolf spoke to my mind once more and the words that I had written before haunted me.

Only in the total darkness of the day can Phoenix raise its head . . . Dark it was; I could scarcely see the fog before me. Suddenly, the cloud moved toward me, glowing with a burst of white from within. Tears ran from my eyes as I thought it would strike me again. The cloud appeared to strike out at me and I rolled to the side to avoid its blow. I jumped to my feet and spoke the words:

"Standing Wolf, take my hand," I said, standing stiff as a tree. I momentarily felt a burning sensation in my stomach, then in an instant a transparent white Wolf leaped from within my chest and appeared on the ground before me. I stumbled and fell backwards about ten feet. The Earth shook once more. Smoke began to rise from the Cotopaxi. The Moon, which had cast its shadow over the sun, was moving to give light to the Earth below once more. The white glow radiated from the center of the fog once more and turned bright red like fire.

I heard a low rumble and then a crack like thunder. Where the white wolf had been standing, a tall Indian man (the one from my dreams), with his old face careworn, materialized in front of me. He threw up his arms and the material from his frock formed a perfect circle. His body blocked a wall of fire that the cloud had thrown toward me. The great fire deflected off the Indian who appeared to be unharmed by its awesome heat and power. A scream came from within the cloud.

"You dare challenge me once more?" the voice bellowed.

The Indian turned to me and reached out his hand toward me. The great crack that had formed in the Earth lay between us. I reached out and took his hand; its warmth was eerie.

"I am the host of your original soul," the Indian yelled. "Return it to me now."

Without warning, we passed through one another, changing places. I then stood between the Indian and the fog.

"Cast out the eye of the Wolf into the fog of blindness," the Indian commanded. "Do not delay!"

I reached into my pocket and retrieved the object that Reeva had given me. I removed the leather strap from the hole within the rock. I drew back my arm and threw the object directly into the center of the cloud. A great burst of air rushed from the cloud and pulled me from my feet. It was not a blowing air but rather a sucking air. A great scream again came from the cloud. I sprang to my feet as I tried in vain to draw a breath. The Earth shook violently.

The glowing white energy formed within the fog once more. The cloud extended into what appeared to be the shape of a claw; it struck me, knocking me to the ground. It left a wound across my neck that bled profusely. Then the fog, as if by a great vacuum from below, was sucked into the massive crack in the Earth.

Dazed, I stood and looked at the Indian. He reached his hand out to me again. I stretched my arm out once more, but I could barely touch his hand over the widening gap in the Earth. As our hands grasped, the massive crack in the Earth began to close, drawing us closer together. Once the massive wound in the Earth was closed, the Indian stared into my eyes.

"Standing Wolf?" I asked, looking at him; I was dizzy from the loss of blood.

"I am he," the Indian said. He reached to the side of his head and removed a dark blue feather. He brushed it over the wound on my neck and the wound disappeared; the pain immediately subsided. Standing Wolf then offered the feather to me; now it was white. I took the feather in my hand. Then, before my eyes, the old Indian man turned into a young warrior, muscular and strong. On the ground beside us lay the white Wolf, covered in blood.

"The Wolf has taken your wound. He has protected you once more," Standing Wolf said.

He reached for my hand once more; I took his grasp. He pulled me across what was the crack in the Earth. As I stood beside him, I looked into his face. A single tear fell from his eye.

"It is over, One of the One," he said. "You can rest now; everything will be just fine." The words gave me comfort.

"I have a lot of questions for you," I demanded. The Indian grinned widely at me.

"Then it is answers you shall have!" Standing Wolf laughed.

As we walked into the woods, my mind raced with everything I wanted to know. I worried that I would ask stupid questions or not ask questions that were really important. Standing Wolf was patient and answered each question without hesitation or comment.

I questioned him about who he was. I questioned him about disease. I questioned him about nuclear weapons and the end of the Earth.

I had been through a lot these past several months, and I wasn't about to get a few lightning bolts in the ass and then walk away empty handed. Things just didn't work that way in my circle.

I heard the voices; I felt the pain; I saw all that was around me. I was consciously aware of everything that was happening to me, but I still have the question in my mind: Did it happen?

Chronicles

I was given the privilege of asking any question I wanted and Standing Wolf, without reservation, gave me the answers—not always the answer that I sought, but an answer that was necessary. Imagine meeting someone who possessed what you perceived to be the answers to every question mankind had and then trying to ask the right questions. There is no way I could have asked the questions that perhaps others would have asked, but at that moment, being totally dumbfounded, I did the best I could and asked what I felt was important.

You will find that Standing Wolf took on somewhat of a sense of humor at this point. He answered every question; and even though I winced after asking some of them, he did not think they were stupid questions and answered as fully as he could and in a way that I would be sure to understand.

Now that I have had a chance to sit back and read the pages that follow, I can think of hundreds of other questions I would have, should have, asked. I can only keep reminding myself of one thing: at least I was given the opportunity to ask.

Question: Why Was I Chosen to Go through All That I Have Been Through in the Past Several Months?

Being "chosen," as you put it, would have been a great honor for many of those before me. You were chosen because of your past experiences. By this I mean the lives that you have led before. Never have you been any other than a champion of your brothers and sisters. You served them well.

I first discussed your coming with the One ninety-seven years before your current birth. The One was very impatient. I, on the other hand, was somewhat doubtful. Your initial contact as a child was well chosen. Though you may not have been conscious of it, a pattern was begun in which your learning process would be staged in such a way that you would absorb things of importance—things that would benefit you in your yet to be undertaken quest.

In your past experiences, you accomplished many things. You were once a teacher of the little ones and you taught them well. Your patience was thin, but nonetheless, you endured. Your teachings sent forth many great chiefs and laid the foundations of a great people.

Your beliefs have not changed much since your first time. You are a stern one today; this I accept. In your times past, you were more open than you are today. You were more receptive to the changes that would come, though you foresaw the perils they would bring. Yours was a wisdom unbridled and the people knew this. You were never chief, but you were one whom many chiefs listened to, sought out, and respected.

You ask why a son of mine was chosen; I ask you in kind, why not? You handled these matters in the manner in which I knew you would, knew was within you. My son set aside his fears, my son set aside his doubts and accepted the challenge of something that was strange to him. My son would only do this because of his thirst for knowledge, his hunger for wisdom, and his desire to learn that which may benefit others.

You sought out the old woman: she who was White Deer of Autumn. Did she teach you anything? Perhaps she only withdrew that which was already within you. This is why I encouraged her and gave her the answers that you sought. She was made to be stagnate for your benefit, to keep her as a device. She will stagnate no more. You will extend my appreciation?

Question: When Will I Die?

There is no death, only a changing of worlds. As far as when it will be time for you to change worlds, I have already given this time to you. The changing of worlds will begin with the breath of the Mother Earth in the nineteen hundred ninety-seventh year. Your calling will necessarily be one of the first. The One of each Thousand will come home first and make ready for the arrival and orientation of the others, none of whom yet have an understanding of who they are or what their destiny will be.

Question: I Have Difficulty Understanding the Concept of the End of the World As People Perceive It. Explain When and How This Will Come to Be.

Compound questions cause me to ramble about much. I have already told you of the Atoll of destruction, that which is controlled by the Great Nation. Its poisons will soon be released and will begin a process that cannot be reversed.

The children of Mother Earth have been poisoning her waters for many years, such that the damage done cannot be repaired. The killing that is taking place as we speak is a vile and detestable act. What brings the tears is the fact that there are many who know of the killings and are keeping it from the people. I do not mean killings of man, I mean killings as of Mother Earth—her waters, her shores, her creatures of innocence, those creatures who are defenseless against man. Man has killed off many species of children that will not be heard from again on this Mother Earth. Do you not think this makes anger within Mother Earth? How does man suppose the Mother Earth feels inside herself when a whole of her children are killed? You have felt it, as have I. The tears come

48

and the tears go, what can be done to return a child once removed? The answer is obvious: nothing.

With the poisoning of the waters comes first the killing of life that has been granted existence within those waters. Next, the life of the shores that depend upon the waters and the creatures who inhabit them. Finally, the killing of the most contemptuous creature who depends upon the waters: man. You would think that man would realize the importance of pure waters, but he shrugs his shoulders in the face of monetary gain. Man cares not about a future he will not attend.

Man dumps his sewage and his garbage into the waters which feed him, give him life. There is not a better definition of a fool. Man dumps the filth of oil into his waters and watches helplessly as the oil attacks all living creatures from above and below. Even man himself is not protected from such destruction. The killing of the fish, the land creatures, and the soils themselves will eventually kill man as well. Nothing, without exception, nothing can exist without pure waters. Man's actions against the waters are contemptible and he should be ashamed of himself. As we speak, no creature that comes from the waters is safe for consumption; all are poisoned and to be consumed requires individual risk. In my original time, all that came from the waters were pure and safe. Our basic instincts told us to keep the waters pure and we did. Man truly deserves the poison.

The signs are there and man is simply not paying attention, but not to be concerned; there is nothing he can do about it anyway. Like an animal that is sick and about to pass, it kicks and shakes and twitches within its own sickness. Mother Earth too is the same way; she kicks and shakes by way of earthquakes and volcanoes. She is about to die, to sleep for a long time. The minor trembles that have been felt in the past were not listened to by man and their damages were little in *comparison to the final shakes to come. To be measured in man's standards would take a Richter scale that reaches or passes thirty. So violent will the shaking be that the rotation about the sun will be severely disturbed. Not until a great shaking returns Mother Earth to her proper place will she begin to heal. Do not feel sorry for those who will be left behind. They deserve the wrath of the kindness and gifts they were heartbound to reject. Let man believe in his own greatness and it will surely be his downfall.*

Question: Who Is the Great Phoenix?

The Great Phoenix is not so much a who as a what. There is nothing great about this entity, which is actually a feeling. Phoenix represents the struggle that exists in the souls of all regarding good and evil, love and hate, question and answer, reason and assumption, lives past, lives present, and life yet to come. When the Phoenix "rises," the conflict within oneself becomes a great destination. The time for the challenging of oneself will preclude all other goals until the challenge is met and conquest attained, on the part of either. One's actions during the challenge and, as you may perceive, the outcome of the conquest is that which will map the next stage for the One.

Phoenix will rise again and again within each, as it has in lives past, as it does in lives present, and as it will in life yet to come—with one exception: Those who challenge their Phoenix and are the victor of the conquest shall face the challenge no more in lives present and life yet to come. Victorious conquest leaves the spirit pure, and a peaceful existence for the remaining stages is the attained result. Fear Phoenix, for Phoenix is fear; doubt Phoenix, for Phoenix is doubt; believe that life is truly a gift and Phoenix will be conquered.

Question: Was My Challenge of the Phoenix Successful?

Ours was the ninth challenge since the conception of our original soul. Your pain is my pain, for there are countless challenges yet to come. I will hold your hand at the time of each challenge, for your challenge is my challenge, and your attempts at conquest are for the benefit of us. Though our hands do not now touch, it is the freedom to explore and the freedom to question that will provide for your best growth. Become your own source of wisdom, learn all that is learnable, and share constantly.

Question: Is There a God?

You struggle with this. As to a "one god" or a "true god," there is not. "God" is a faith and a belief that is different in all peoples; no two people share the same type of faith; no two people share the same type of belief. God is the faith and belief that exists in all that provides guidance, direction, and purpose. When we ask of ourselves, the answer is always there. Some refer to this as instinct and not faith, belief, or God. When one prays to a god, one is actually seeking one's own soul. The prayer is like the joining of oneself; it is the instillment of confidence; it is the selection of reasoning; it is the power from within to move forward.

When a prayer is thought to a god, be it directed to a figure, an imaginary spirit, as in raising one's arms to the sky, this is harmless. This practice instills good feeling in many— just as the peoples choose to congregate in a house of worship, it is harmless. The sharing of the seeking of confidence in one's existence and the sharing of the seeking of the power from within is a bonding of the peoples. This is the finest shield against that which is considered evil in the hearts of the peoples. The bonding, the joining, and the congregating of the people is a beautiful experience and is best shared.

Question: The House of Worship You Refer to, the Church, What Is Its Purpose? If All People Have the Power of a God Within, Why Is It Necessary?

The house of worship, the church, has been explained. A common place to gather and search one's soul is harmless. Those who have the need to congregate in one place with others in order to be able to call upon the power and the good from within are justified in doing so. Some need the support of others to justify the seeking of one's soul, one's inner power, and the search for the answers they desire. The "church on Sunday" rule can stifle the soul. The soul, the self being, is a wonderful thing that should be conferred with constantly, and not once a week.

Question: When Will Organized Religion Fall?

It already has. Organized religion has become monetary. Many have found that the "religion" found within oneself is the best religion and no longer feel the need to pay for the joy of seeking the God within. The good which is provided to many through organized religion should not be cast aside. Many benefits come from the organization of the hearts and the souls of people. The portion of organized religion which is malevolent is the amassing of monetary gains which serve no purpose other than this statement.

Question: Who Are the Most Perfect Children?

The most perfect children are those of all ages who have learned to live in peaceful coexistence with all people and who bear no ill will toward others. Those who are happy in knowing who they are, for they are self, and what they are, for they are self. My warning is explicit, the perfect children ignore the Phoenix and he strikes at their hearts with a blood-letting that can kill them all should they seek not their roots of contention. The perfect children cry out in pain for a champion. We are that champion and will appoint others to support their burden. Time is short for us; speak loud, speak strong, speak now! Our tears have fallen and will fall further like a great river. Sympathy is not sought; action is. The most perfect children are those who came here first; those who brought the knowledge and the idea; those who respect Mother Earth not only for who she is but for the knowledge of why she does what she does for her children.

Question: How Do People Know If They Have Lived a Past Life or If They Are an Original Soul?

It is the simple recalling of something one has done, seen, experienced or heard of before. It is the continuance, the passing of one existence to the next, and the proof sought that people are destined to live a life over and over again, supposedly until they get it right. Each person has but one task to "get right" during their existence; this is the challenging of Phoenix as explained to us before. Until the challenge is met and until conquest is attained, the soul cries to Mother Earth for yet another chance. Mother Earth is a kind and generous bosom and grants the request for the chance to challenge and to realize the gift of life, without hesitation. With all her goodness, it should be no wonder that she is about to strike back. There are times when you will remember the past lives, not entirely but in part. You will question these remembrances and then accept. In order to be welcoming and understanding of the remembrances, one must first be awakened.

Question: What Is the Meaning of Life?

You are still confused, my son. There is no meaning of life. This is a trick question, but one that deserves to be answered. Life is a gift, as if a granting. Life is something that is given and it is yours to do with as you wish. Life asks nothing of you except for this understanding. Unlike all other things which I bid you to question, the one thing one should never question is a gift. Your existence is a gift like any other, one you may do with what you wish. Using the gift in a wise and understanding way will make sure the giver of the gift will continue to give for much time to come.

Question: Who Is Mother Earth?

Mother Earth is that from which all is born.

Question: Explain Mother Earth.

Mother Earth is that from which all is born.

Question: Is Mother Earth This Planet We Live On?

Mother Earth is that from which all is born.

Question: Is There Any Truth in the Big Bang Theory?

The big bang theory is erroneous on its face, but its meaning contains much wisdom. The planets were once contained as one. Their great dividing sent them to certain resting points. The essence contained in the One were spread far and wide to begin again. An exploding universe is not as fictional as those—mostly those of religion—would believe. Crediting one man or one god for all creation is fiction. However, crediting one man or one god for giving direction, purpose, and meaning is not, as long as it is believed that the one god exists within.

Question: Is There Life on Other Planets?

There are countless thousands of Mother Earths which exist throughout all eternity, that which is referred to as a universe or a galaxy.

Question: Is There Life on Any of the Planets That Have Been Charted by the People of Earth, Those Planets That We All Know Of?

Yes.

Question: What Is the "Source"?

Mother Earth.

Question: Who Is Providing the Answers to My Questions?

We are.

Question: Who Are "We"?

We are the collective souls of those previously visited. We are the knowledge and the wisdom attained through many challenges past and we are the forethought of the challenges yet to come. We are aware of our existence and we are aware of our meaning. We are the spiritual and the physical joined through mutual experience. We are the containment of the answers sought by many. We are the birth of the northern lands and we are the continuance of the veracity of the fallen attempts of many. We are that which carries on the journey of souls in their quest for purpose. We are One of the One. The planets which were once contained as one spawned few offspring. You, the physical, and I, the spiritual, are the "we." We are the last incarnates of the remaining original soul. We are the Lojon, the father, the One of the One.

I am Standing Wolf; he who stands firm; he who is the protector; incarnate of Running Wolf; he who was the seeker of all that I knew. You are Anthony, he who is like God but not; incarnate of Standing Wolf, who, like the Lojon, lives again and again. Your incarnate, who has not yet been named, is he who seeks you now and learns from you now. All that you know, all that you see, all that you do will become available for his wisdom. Lojon is the first host of your original soul. I have lived since the beginning and am the existence that will never cease to exist.

Question: What Will Be Left of Mother Earth after the Predicted Tumultuous Destruction to Come?

We have made no such prediction.

Others have predicted the destruction of certain portions of the Earth through earthquakes, volcanos and the like; this is what I mean by the tumultuous predicted destruction to come.

The Earth shakes predicted by the great minds are far from their mark on many and on the target on few. Shifting of the surface has been a continuing occurrence since separation. The pores, or fault lines, are predicted in close proximity to their actual existence. The peoples would take well heed to avoid these areas. Their presence is placing a great pressure upon these wounds, and the development and destruction which occurs in and around them will surely cause the lands to separate prematurely.

The testing of weaponry underground in the northern lands has caused much damage, damage which is beyond repair. The leaders of the great nation will be the downfall of their own lands. More than half the northern lands will be lost under the waters, which will displace them. This displacement will cause the lowering of the waters in other areas and the unveiling of new lands as well as the suffering of those lands which depend upon the water level where it shores now. The time will come when the midwestern plains of the northern lands will experience the Earth shakes, the tidal waves, and the wrath of the moving waters. The eastern plains will experience a great dipping toward the midwestern lands and the unveiling of new lands worthy of inhabitants.

The cessation of existence caused by the shifting of the lands will be surmountous. Heed the season of occurrence; it be winter, when the peoples are ill prepared.

Question: What Will Become of the Survivors of This Destruction?

Rebirth.

Question: Where Does the Spirit Go After the Physical Life Has Ended?

Immediate rebirth or immediate finality. The life cycle resumes upon demand of the spirit or remains in limbo until called upon by the incarnate, or Mother Earth, when ready. Many spirits travel to other Mother Earths before they begin again. This purpose is for the sharing of knowledge, which, upon rebirth, is actually wisdom. All Mother Earths allow their children to progress at their own pace. Even in your time of erroneous technology, peoples of other Mother Earths have not changed since their beginning and live as you once did.

Question: Is There a Cure for Cancer?

The cure lies in the beginning, the birth, self-help, self-care, self-wisdom, self-knowing. The cure lies in the prevention. Cancer, like immuno-deficiencies, is a manmade disease. As prevention is the best remedy, the cure for those already afflicted is known and has been known for some time. This cure is withheld by the leaders of the great nation.

Cancer is self-inflicted; cancer is monetary. Cancer is the rotting of one's soul, beginning with the flesh. The answer will come with the challenge, when the champion takes up the cause and forces the truth. Mother Earth cannot cure that which she does not cause. Manmade is man cured.

Question: Why Are People Born with Handicaps?

Those born without hope, as special peoples, are born so in punishment for deeds in past lives. This lifetime is the one that must be lived in punishment so that the lives yet to be had can again be fruitful and beneficial to the soul and the spirits around it.

Do not scorn their birth, as all souls in some rebirthing must experience the same pain. We are the choosing of our own destined pain. This life is the cleansing of the path for the beautiful lives yet to come. Joy at their birthing; you should know there are better lives for them ahead.

Question: How Can We, the Inhabitants, Best Help Mother Earth Survive?

All that was necessary for survival in the living in peace and harmony and the oneness in each other was provided in the beginning. The lust of the people for things greater than sustenance requires has caused damages beyond repair. The raping of the lands and the inquisitiveness that lies beneath them, the polluting of the skies and the shield of the sun, the poisoning of the waters are a direct cause of all that is monetary. Man's quest for monetary gain will be his downfall. Only through the pending downfall of the monetary system will the peoples be forced to return to the ways of the beginning. Those who are left, those who will be few, will know this and prevent reoccurrence. The monetary system, which is mankind's way of holding itself above its own, is the greatest atrocity set forth by Phoenix. When mankind no longer feels the need to fight for superiority over his own, the amassing of riches greater than his own, and the need to govern over the many for the benefit of the few, the self, will the Mother Earth's tears be dried.

Question: What Is Happening to the Ozone Layer?

Man has punched many holes in this protective shield in his quest for dominance and control. The ozone layer is being destroyed for monetary gain. The damage caused so far is irreparable. The shield against the sun cannot repair itself, and there is no possibility that man can stop the gap he has created. The openings will cause more than a burning upon Mother Earth. The openings will lend aid to the shifting of Mother Earth off her southern feet. A further result will be the melting of the frozen tear and massive flooding, the most devastating results reared upon the northwestern lands.

Mother Earth provided what created and maintained the shield and man is destroying it. The shame is that man knows he is doing it and has known for some time. Only now are the peoples beginning to learn of the destruction and the devastation to come. The damage cannot be reversed but can be prevented from worsening. As far as the outcome of the damage, it will happen regardless of what man does. Believe not that there is no hope. The final days can still be lived in relative harmony and an inner feeling of safety, but the outcome is still inevitable. Just how much does man think one Mother Earth can take?

Question: Does Everyone Face Phoenix in the Same Manner in Which I Faced Phoenix?

No. Our contact was selected; our contact was physical. Other contacts are like a challenge of one's soul from within. Others have met the physical challenge of Phoenix; none have succeeded as failure is the general rule. Sadly, without the challenges of Phoenix, there is little reason for existence.

Question: Will There Be a Third World War?

That which you call a world war, and the third of its kind, has already occurred. A world war is a war in which all or a majority of the peoples of the world are involved. This war took place in the cities of oil.

Question: Will Nuclear Weapons Be Used in the Future?

Nuclear "accidents" will occur as a direct result of the attempted destruction of the weapon, the impatient destruction of the weapon of dominance. Many accidents have already occurred. The leaders of the great nation have hidden many accidents from the peoples and the inhabitants of the Earth. The leaders of the great nation have killed, are killing, and will kill more of their peoples through error than in all past wars combined. These killings have occurred, are occurring, and will continue to occur in secret.

Question: Why Do You Target the Great Nation and Its Monetary Goals So Readily?

The leaders of the Great Nation seek monetary gains and will stop at nothing, even the slaughter of their own peoples through war, pestilence, starvation, taxation, and more, to attain their goals. Those who replace them are of the same kindred spirit. The guise of a people living free is a falsehood. Nowhere, even in your known communist countries, are there more laws against the peoples than in the Great Nation—laws designed to keep the peoples downtrodden, poor, and under control. The Great Nation has appointed as assassins of the peoples' mere existence an agency without law, an agency without control, and an agency that may violate even the most precarious of laws designed for whatever purpose to see to it that this goal is reached, and that those who govern may continue to freely rape and pillage their own electorate, under the guise of a free vote that can be repealed by a select few.

The governing of the Great Nation has reached its peak and will fall prey to those to whom it freely gave. After the Earth shakes have settled, the smaller lands will fall prey to easy domination.

Question: What Is the Cause of AIDS?

This virus of no immunity is a manmade weapon that failed and did not produce the results for which it was intended. It is a virus unleashed and has grown outside the proportions of understanding. Stupidity caused the infliction; ignorance allows it to grow. The virus is a study. Only Mother Earth could cure this disease, but she would need the help and the understanding of those in agriculture. The shifting of growth priorities would have to be undertaken, and the profits would be little; therefore it would never happen. A common plea of humanity will necessitate the agriculturists' undertaking of an unprofitable assistance to the unwanted. Manmade is man-cured, but in this instance, Mother Earth will protect her most perfect children. In the alfalfa fields: strip its leaves and stew it in a tea, brew it strong, sweeten it not, dilute it not, drink of it in mass quantities and consume of its bitter derivative. Begin at the onset of the positive testing and continue until the final rest is granted. Existence unsaved, yet existence granted.

Question: When Will Be the Final Day of Earth?

*When the sun dies an Aquarian death, in the year 3988.
Mother Earth shall rehabitate with the education of the new
child in a thousand years times seven.*

Question: Oil Slicks on the Oceans and Seas Plague Mother Earth Now. Is There a Method of Better Ridding Her Waters of the Poison?

Poison is the true word. Its only cure lies in the depletion of its fossilized derivative, but Mother Earth will rest before this happens. Once these poisons are unleashed against the waters of Mother Earth, they can never be removed. The poison's presence may be eventually removed visually, but its effects are permanent.

Question: What Was or Is Atlantis?

The home soil. The name given to the first settlement of a sister planet by those before their time who were destroyed by their admission of superiority. The unknown war of Atlantis created its total destruction, rendering searches fruitless. Atlantis, as it is called, did exist, but it was long before the first indigenous peoples.

Question: Explain the Contents of the Bible. What Is the Meaning of Revelations?

This is the question whose answer most peoples fear. The writings to which you refer are the compilations of the actions and prophecies of a man called Jesus. Many have mistaken the writings as the works of "God." The man Jesus was purported to be the son of God. This is an impossibility as discussed previously; "God" is an entity that exists within us all. The man Jesus could have been the son of any man who was aware of the god within. Like your writings, the writings of Jesus were not done by him but rather for him. The writers were the prophets, or the seers. The prophets kept the chronicles of Jesus and wrote of his actions, his sayings, and his stories of things to come.

Many wrote their own versions of what they thought was said, what they thought they heard, what they thought they saw. These were not writings that Jesus sat down and read for approval.

The Bible is a large volume of writings; many versions consist of nearly or over a thousand pages. Like the religious leaders of the present who order their prophecies catalogued and written, so then, in his time, did the man called Jesus.

The prophecies of Jesus, as originally intended, are the most widely followed today. As was done then at the time of the original writings, and is widely done today, the writings of Jesus have been interpreted by many different religions and rewritten or edited to fit certain religious beliefs. As with the writers of the prophecies of Jesus, such as Job, Samuel, Daniel, Malachi, and so on, in the Old Testament, and Mark, Luke, John, Peter, and so on, in the New Testament, to each person the words had different meaning. As with the writers of the original Bible, these were not necessarily the words, actions, or teachings of the man Jesus, but these were the thoughts of the writers as to what the words, actions, or teachings of the man they followed meant.

In his time, filled with much strife, mayhem, and general unrest in a new beginning, a man like Jesus was revered as someone who was all-knowing and all-powerful. He was someone people could look up to, and for the times, this was good.

The actions credited to Jesus in the writings have never been verified and undoubtedly never will be. It is not known whether Jesus actually fed the masses, as is suggested by Matthew in the New Testament. Was this the writing of Matthew as he witnessed it? Or was this the writing of Matthew as it was told to him by one of the countless thousands who were in attendance at the reported miracle of five loaves?

After the feast of the masses, Matthew further writes of Jesus having walked on water. His disciples had left the area by boat while Jesus was praying in the mountains. Upon finishing the prayer, Jesus was reported to have walked on water toward the boat. By the same token, one of the disciples, Peter, was said to have walked on the water as well as he left the boat to meet Jesus. This was supposed to have been done with the assistance of Jesus.

Further, the reported miracle of Jesus changing water into wine was suggested by John in the New Testament. Jesus attended a wedding and the upper-class attendees wanted wine to drink but had none. Jesus was reported to have changed six stone waterpots filled with water into wine. The ruler of the feast drank of the contents of the stone pots and found it to be wine; but there is no reference that Jesus made this happen. The only reference is that the governor of the feast did not know where the wine came from, but that the servants who filled the pots with water did know where it came from. These writings regarding the changing of water into wine, which occurred at the marriage in Cana, end by declaring the wine a miracle; no credit was actually given to Jesus for it.

These are the most popular Biblical references in the minds of peoples in times present, as they are the most repeated miracles that were to have happened.

The report of Jesus and the Spirit, God, having come from the heavens itself is truth, as the heavens are the place from where all people began. This is not to insinuate that Jesus or God was alien in nature, but certainly any man, or entity, who can appear on Earth and garner multitudes of followers in such a day and age certainly had an influence, and a strong influence at that, since it still controls many to this date. In the time of Jesus, not only was universal travel to and from faraway places possible, but travel to a land of unknowing people was quite frequent.

There were those, even in Jesus' time, that refused to follow him and doubted his veracity. Jesus was stoned and then crucified by the very people he was supposed to lead. Jesus was reported to have risen from the dead, but then, so were others such as Lazarus and Dorcas. In order for a god to be a god, the entity must be all knowing, all forgiving, all loving; and within each of us, these qualities exist. But in Exodus, God is described as a jealous man; this is not possible of a purported "true god." There is the justice of God, the knowledge of God, the love of God, the mercy of God, God the omnipotent, God the omnipresent, the perfection of God, the personality of God, the power of God, the presence of God, the providence of God, the righteousness of God, the unchangeable and unsearchable God, the wisdom of God, God the spirit—compare each of these meanings and you will know that they are not possible.

There are those who I would label as false prophets, those who declare that God is monetary and that followers must give of money in order to have anything to do with God. Of all the gods declared above, never, even in the purported writings of Jesus, was monetary amassment a necessity for the miracles that were supposedly done. A true god would not be monetary. You would not pay yourself to seek the soul, the spirit, the self contained within each of us.

The Bible is a mere compilation of what men, at the time of its writing, truly believed. The fact that there are many who truly believe it to this date is harmless, just so the belief does not convince each believer that there is not a god within oneself. Once a belief in a book of writings replaces the belief in oneself, then the true soul, the true spirit, is lost forever.

Nowhere in the Bible does it prove that the spirit God or Jesus performed any miracle that each of us cannot perform for ourselves. Nowhere do the writings suggest that they are perfect, without flaw; and nowhere do the writings suggest that they are the only true words. As many would phrase it today, either Jesus was real and the writings he caused are fact, or he was no different than those prophets of today. The only difference would be that Jesus may have wanted people to believe in one god, a spirit god, which is not possible, but he had no special powers to make it so.

Revelations, or the Apocalypse, is the predictions of Jesus' writers of things to come. They are not intended to be predictions of the near future, but rather of the distant future. Armageddon and the second coming are the most famed of the predictions. If the lore contained within Revelations were to be carefully deciphered, a good estimate of the second coming, coupled with Armageddon, would also be the year 3988. However, why would a god purported to be so good come back for no other reason than to destroy the world?

Revelations appears intended to put the proverbial fear of God into the people, or a last ditch attempt to say: "If you don't follow the teachings in the Bible, look what will happen to you." No happening or occurrence since the original writings, more than two thousand years ago, has been proven to parallel the predictions of Revelations.

The Bible is a story well told in its original form, which over the years has been altered to a point of near total rewriting. The Bible has been interpreted by many, mostly organized religion, and construed to mean exactly what each religion wants it to mean to its followers. This is like any other writing; its interpretation is left solely to the reader, whose own interpretation can never be wrong.

Jesus had at least one unmistakable quality: through his teachings and beliefs, the people were rallied and came together for a common cause. Since his time, millions of people have followed his teachings and have found peace within themselves from them; this is good. The warning has been given: No teaching is beneficial that prompts an individual to fail to seek out his or her inner spirit, inner soul, inner God.

I share these beliefs with you at your insistence. We believe in the spirit within and that belief cannot be broken in us. As long as we have faith in ourselves, love one another equally and hold contempt for no one person for no one reason, then we are content and are doing no more than those who would teach these ways would truly ask that we do.

This book is only fiction to those who question its validity or truly do not believe. To those who do believe, it is placed above all truth and becomes words to rearrange, words to hold over others, and words to live by, or cease to exist without.

Question: Are There Aliens on Earth?

Specify.

Question: Are There Aliens from Other Planets within or without Our Solar System Who Are Visiting or Living on Earth?

"Alien" is a term used by people to describe others who are different from them. The term could be used by a black man when describing a white man, or used by a female when describing a male. Alien simply means foreign or strange, or unfortunately the most popular, hostile. There are no aliens; all who are here belong here.

To ask if there are beings from other Mother Earths who have visited this Mother Earth: yes, there are. To ask if there are beings from other Mother Earths who are living on this Mother Earth; there are. These other beings, or children, are not hostile.

This Mother Earth is the last of the original planets to evolve. Its peoples have not yet reached the evolutionary scale of many of the offspring of the One. For others to come to this Mother Earth to live is similar to the North American space program; it is a challenge to venture to a different place.

Remember, all that sprang from the original One is the same. Life on other Mother Earths is the same as life on this Mother Earth with minor evolutionary differences that compensate for their location. Each planet revolves around its own nova, or sun. There are nearly 2,000 other planets capable of sustaining life as it is on this Mother Earth, should her inhabitants evolve to the stage where they can travel there—but this time is exactly one thousand eight hundred and seven years away. There are those on your Mother Earth who now dream of such travels, but dreams are all they will be in your lifetime.

The living Mother Earths in this solar system—Earth, Mercury, and Venus—all contain some form of life, this is known, the Earth being the most advanced of the three. The dead planets—Mars, Jupiter, Saturn, Uranus, Neptune, and Pluto—are asteroidal and support no life forms.

Those beings from other Mother Earths now on this Mother Earth are not from this universe. Many travel here by supportive means; many travel here by spiritual means. Children from other Mother Earths have lived on the Mother Earth since its beginning. Remember, they are of the one true Mother Earth; all life is derived from the one true Mother Earth.

The largest influx of beings from other Mother Earths to this Mother Earth occurred in two separate stages. The first stage was the Earth year 1326, the year of the destruction of the eighteenth sun. Nearly seventy million children began the long journey to this Mother Earth. It pains in my heart to say, barely a tenth survived the journey. Even in this time, the journey took only the equivalent of eleven Earth years. The second stage was sporadic, between the years 1907 and 1964. The largest settled areas were on the southern continents. Many actually travel backwards in time to reach this Mother Earth and are introduced as orphans, adoptive children, or those since passed on—most are female.

As of this date there are approximately thirty-one million people living on this Mother Earth who traveled from or sprang from other Mother Earths. Modern day people often fear the very "aliens" they have been living with for nearly seven hundred years.

After the year 2951, beings from other Mother Earths will cease to journey to this Mother Earth, for they will know of her pending destruction.

Question: Explain Relativity.

What you truly seek is the explanation of why all that exists does exist. All that exists is related by having come from the same source: Mother Earth.

Question: Why Is There Homosexuality? Is It an Illness? Are People Born Homosexual or Do They Become Homosexual? Why Are Homosexual and Other Types of People Discriminated Against?

A homosexual is a person of either sex whose sexual tendencies lean towards members of the same sex. Homosexual tendencies are instilled in the womb. Homosexuality is not an illness; these men and women are functioning, contributing members of society. "Homosexual" is not the person they are, it is the sexual tendencies they are given in the womb.

Labeling homosexuals is like labeling people as Jew, Hispanic, Irish, English, or to label them by a disease or skin color. Man thrives on relating to people who are different than he as inferior. Homosexuals refer to nonhomosexuals as "straight," which is construed as an admission that they themselves (homosexuals) are not straight; thus they portray themselves as different or abnormal.

Each society either looks down upon or up to other societies. All people are the same inside, in the heart. All people breathe the same air, require the same foods for survival, and basically function like everyone else. The only real difference in all people is shameful: their descriptive languages used to identify each other.

In the natural evolution, when one animal depends on the consumption of another for survival, the consumed animal is bred in large numbers. Unlike heterosexuals, who reproduce and keep the population growing, homosexuals do not reproduce and keep the population at a constant. Those who do reproduce, and produce those who do not, do so for a reason. If all humans reproduced, Mother Earth would not be able to sustain them. All that comes from Mother Earth contains her wisdom and instructions. Mother Earth knows how many people she can sustain, how many animals she can

88

sustain, how much plant life she can sustain. When plant life chokes its own environment, nature does not permit the necessary cross pollination. When the population of Mother Earth swells, she does not permit reproduction, or causes reproduction to slow down.

Homosexuals do not reproduce, which would further endanger the staggering population, the environment, and so on. Homosexuals, timid and kind in nature, hold no ill will for the most part for any other, except those who may attack or brutalize them. Procreation is a natural occurrence among human beings. Heterosexual tendencies are also a natural occurrence; so are homosexual tendencies. I can question you to create thought: If procreation is natural, and we know that homosexual tendencies occur in the womb, why would heterosexual people give birth to homosexual people if homosexuality were not a natural part of evolution?

Just as those who reproduce have a function on Mother Earth, so do those who do not.

Question: What Is the "Third Eye"?

The "third eye," as you refer to it, is believed by many to be one's ability to see the future. Since all peoples control their own destinies, all peoples have a third eye.

The opening of the third eye is done each time we plan the simplest tasks: cooking dinner, mapping out a vacation route, making an appointment to visit a doctor, having an automobile repaired, or having our hair done. The third eye is the sixth sense.

Question: Why Is There Starvation in Selected Parts of the World?

Those who do not feed upon Mother Earth are fed upon by her. Those areas of the world that have such a plague are over populated for the life the area was intended to sustain. This same starvation not only attacks human life, but animal life and plant life as well. When the animal hungers, he attacks the plant; when the human hungers, he attacks the animal. The cycle remains constant. Mother Earth is again controlling the number of peoples she can sustain. Remember, there is no monetary gain in feeding the hungry or helping the less fortunate.

Question: Why Is There Illness and Disease among the People When We Have the Medical Technology to Cure Most Anything? If the Medical Technology Is Not There, Why Was It Not Brought by Those from Other Planets Who Live Here Now?

A cure for everything is provided by Mother Earth, so long as the affliction is also caused by Mother Earth and so long as it is the will of Mother Earth that it be cured.

In their quest for advancement and superiority, humans are the largest predator of themselves through technology and advancement. Such technologies and advancements are not required to sustain life upon Mother Earth.

Question: In the Great Nation, the Economy Is in Poor Shape. This Is Monetary, I Know, but Being from the Great Nation, I Am Naturally Curious. Many Predict Devastating Effects as a Result of the Troubled Economy in America. What Will Happen?

Though the Great Nation has always been in a depression for countless millions, a depression for all will emerge after the election of a Democratic president to lead the Great Nation. The election will be found to not have been fair.

The government of the Great Nation and its businesses will be subject to international interference. Those who have been helped most by the Great Nation will take the greatest advantage of her upheaval. Much is being done now to plan the destruction of the Great Nation.

A great president, however, is coming soon, not within your lifetime but soon. Before it falls, the Great Nation will become a divided nation of three.

Question: There Is a Lot of Unrest Overseas, in Europe and in Many Religious Countries. Why Is It That These People Cannot Get Along? If I Am to Believe That All of Mother Earth's Children Are the Same, Then I Have a Problem Understanding What Is Happening.

Many want others to live their ways and according to their rules. Many seek power who would abuse it if attained. Many believe as they have been taught that their religion is just and that others who will not follow it must suffer beneath it. Jealousy and prejudice are abundant in cultures that are ignorant to the true meaning of the grand creation, cultures that actually spurn its ideals and the possibility of its meaning being real.

Who is the strongest? Who is the greatest? Who is going to ultimately be able to rule over others? These are questions that the unrest is designed to answer, but the answers will not come.

Question: I Have Heard So Many Different Explanations about Why We Are Beginning to Have So Many Earthquakes. Is There a Reason for Them? And Why Are There So Many of Them Now?

It is not just the rumbling earthquakes that are taking place; there is so much more. Many changes are taking place on this Mother Earth and in the skies above her.

The waters are lost; this you have seen. I wish for you to meet one of my sons who will show you her beauty as it was, but for now, Mother Earth is in disgust.

The earthquakes are setting a pattern, one that cannot be seen, for the pattern is deep within her. The pattern is like the making of a puzzle: until all the pieces are cut, it is incomplete and cannot be dismantled before one tries to reassemble it again. The earthquakes are laying the pattern of the rebirths to come, but as you have seen, the rebirths cannot take place until Mother Earth has rid herself of her unworthy children. The earthquakes will allow for the swallowing whole of them all. Count the lives taken and keep a record. They be small, for now.

The skies that are the keepers of the air you breathe are only now reaching the full poisonous level necessary to make even a once life-giving breath a destroyer, poisoned them they have. The burning of rocks, the puffing of the chemicals, both known and in secret—the greedy few are following Mother Earth's well-laid plan. Of course they may do these things to the skies, but for their greed and the profits they reap they will suffocate in their own filthy breath.

I have bored you to the point of disgust regarding the poisoning of the waters, but now all three have fallen, the water, the land, and the skies. What more can man do to himself? The child's punishment for these deeds will be treacherous. In all the knowledge that mankind has of the damage he has done, know that he will still fall in amazement and ask, why? Then there will be those of us who will laugh in shame. Mankind knows why but his greed has made reason come too late.

Let them sleep with blackened lungs and skin of fire. Let them see through eyes that bleed. Let them live short lives with flesh that rots from within. Will they still ask why then? Yes, they will.

Question: The Puzzle, I Assume Someone Will Be Around to Try to Put It Back Together. But Who, and How Will It Be Possible?

Perhaps I have not been as clear on this as I should. This is not the first time around for mankind on this Mother Earth. It is the first time around for this species but not this Mother Earth. Traces of a before time have been found all over Mother Earth. They are always found deep within her, just as she swallowed them whole, just as she will do again.

The spirits and souls of those who will evolve again, the One of each Thousand that I have spoken much of, will come to her again. In time they will find the traces of a before time too, and those traces will be of your time and a short time yet to come. The circle will continue to form, just as it has since the days of the One.

If mankind could go deep within Mother Earth, which is not permitted, he would see traces of a before time that once was known as the first sun, the first day, and the vision of the spirits and souls of the first day would be truly ugly to the people of the now time. Imagine what the faces will look like in the far times to come. Man thinks himself beautiful now; he has not and will not see the beauty of the spirits and souls to come.

The days will come when the children will not require the lands and the skies and the waters. Mother Earth knows this and she makes her children ready and wise. But that time is far to come, and mankind will not see it; but you will, my son, and I will be there to guide you as I do today. This will be the greatest challenge indeed. Does this not bring a smile to your heart? The compassion, in spite of the hunger to come, that will be shown?

Question: Why Are the People of Mother Earth Divided Now? I Ask This in Terms of Countries and Races.

Like the animals who are in their places and no other, so is mankind. All over Mother Earth, man brings animals that do not belong and displays them as great prizes. There is no lesson learned in this.

Mankind is in its place as well, but moves freely. Too often mankind does not return to where from he came from. Mother Earth knew where the souls would be, but the spirit of each grew restless and yearned for places elsewhere. Mankind found in the other places, other peoples, many of whom lacked his knowledge and benefits. Mankind thought these were people to be lead, bought, sold, ruled, and tormented, and did well to perform this task and performs this task still.

Mankind still does not accept the message of responsibility given. Instead, he listens to himself and reveres the power that he thinks he has. As long as there are others to torment and cause to lose face in his presence, mankind will continue with his dominating ways. The single largest abuser of the message is the Great Nation, her peoples, because they follow a government most heinous.

So you realize that the people were divided through a plan laid with care and mankind himself disrupted that plan. Man should keep his nose to the grindstone rather than in the homes and places of others. These would be good teachings if only the great white man would listen, but he does not hear words of wisdom well.

I remember my first time when you were yet spoken of, all were the same. All had their place; all had their respon-

sibility; all had their required knowledge. The downfall of my time was in the spiriting from our home. If you decide within yourself that you do not need your home or want your home, then why have it?

Question: The White Wolf Who Came to Me As a Child—What Was His Purpose?

"Her" purpose was more of an interest and a test. The purpose was to bring forth the vision of the seed to come and to present it to the One. It was fed to your Phoenix that it be ready for your coming.

It represented that you had no fear of the visions you saw, that you stood fast and looked with much question. It represented that your independence was intact at that young age and could only grow stronger in the days to come. It represented that you could not be driven from where you stood, as such a sighting would have sent most of your years fleeing.

I was proud at heart that you stood fast. I must admit to you that I lacked the conviction of the One in your choosing. You had much to learn and had many dreams between your ears. Laugh with me now for my pride lacks an apology for my error. I am no different from you.

Question: When My Physical Life Ends, Will I Still Be a Part of What Comes after That?

In many ways. When your physical existence ends you are chosen to take my place and lead the next of the chosen Ones. You will see the visions of the youth, the learning, and the growing until the day of contact.

Question: How Will I Know Who the Next Chosen One Is?

He has already been selected and in fact, you have already met him. You should remember his vision when you stood at the western waters and bellowed at them, "I am the Wolf, what do you think about that?" I see the surprise in your face, my son. I, though always at your side, do not always make my presence known to you. I smiled with you and then sent him your way.

You may not recall his face now, but when you lay your hand upon his shoulder, as did I with you, you will remember him. Much like the Wolf appeared to you as a child and momentarily piqued your interest, you appeared before him and piqued his interest.

He did not think you strange; he thought you bold in the presence of others. He thought you courageous to stand against the mighty ocean. He thought you wise to ask a question of one who clearly could not answer. He does not remember you now, but in the next plane, he will have the recollection of the vision unseen by the eyes he will then possess.

Question: Was I Chosen before Birth or After?

Long before this birth. Your seed was planted on the day of the first sun, as were many others. You have been as long as there has been sun, as long as there have been waters to cause you to sprout again and again.

Question: Is There Anything You Wish Me to Know from These Experiences That I Have Not Yet Questioned You About?

Much.

Your inquisitiveness on the mountain was genuine and succinct. The One had chosen you well. As we walked the wooded trails, your sorrows, though well protected, were abundant. You grieve unlike any other, not for those passed, not for things passed, but for those who are and for things that are. Your concern for mankind and this world is immeasurable. You have tried to ask of us that which is considered to be important to all—this is noble. What you fail to ask is the simple, that which many deem to be meaningless but that which carries the greatest of messages.

Your first encounter with the Wolf as a child was an instilled memory. This was your introduction to your soul as a child, pure, white, innocent. The Wolf had come from my confrontation, the confrontation in which I would be prisoner. The Wolf gave to you at that time the message needed, the imprint of the mold that would give realization and direction to your existence. That which was imprinted upon your memory gave essence to that which you are now. The kindness, hidden and genuine, that you project toward all who exist—be they human, be they animal, be they grown—is a trait instilled and nurtured to maturity.

You were hardened as a child; much of this was necessary for the day you would face the physical challenge would be the greatest challenge you would ever endure. The dawning of the dreams, the awakening of the spirit within, was a chosen time. Verse was made known to you that you might question its validity with all your heart; and to any man, the answers should not have come, but to you . . . As you guessed as a child, thought possible as a boy, and now know as a man,

man's rape of the land, of the self worth of others, and of himself will be his own nemesis.

Allow me to speak freely to your mind and listen much. I will tell you of the things to come, things that will come, and of those who will doubt that which you will speak of.

Remember, mankind does not believe in the young, but I will believe in you for them. If you will but open your heart to me, I will fill it, and in its filling, the compassion and the tears will surround you, perhaps embitter you. As are all of my sons before me, with me, and yet to come, you are strong-willed and will find the way from within yourself to accept.

As we continued to walk, Standing Wolf spoke of many things that were of interest and some that were not. I had to remember that though some things were not important to me, they were to others; and though mine were the only ears to hear it, mine are not the only eyes that will see it.

In this present, and beginning with the mother of the communist republics, the tumbling of governments will strike a doubtful fear in the minds of all. The Great Nation shall not be the last to fall; her ruling nemesis shall bear a scepter. As the governed regain control of themselves and their lands, the governments will threaten and attempt to strike out militarily, but the armies, who are also governed peoples, will abstain.

The smallest of nations will fall prey to the Great Nation, as she forgives her own indebtedness and balks at the angry cries. They will fall in specific orders: Russian, German, African, French, the Nations of Oil, the Nations of Eastern Religions. The Mediterranean Sea will dry up and its shores as well. All of North America will fall as a whole, beginning with the succession of the pacific paradise from her adoptive mother. The Red Nation will smile. The bitterness of the Atoll of the Great Nation will be released, and the destruction of the pacific waters will eventually globalize. The Mexican lands and the Central Americas, Canada will be the most ill prepared. Her southern sister will be too engulfed in civil upheaval to assist. South America will sustain itself longer than most, but not as long as Australia, which will divide itself through tremors from the Timor Sea into two separate nations, but one people, she will endure. Then, Japan and the countries of little notice in the north and south will fall, then the United Kingdom and her holdings; however, her methods will remain constant.

The island nations will survive the turmoil, only because their numbers are few. The last to fall will be China. Her peoples will traverse their borders in search of that which they will not find.

The peoples will be governed in mass no longer. Heed the time for it is now. Heed the heightened awareness, for it is the time of the greatest rising of Phoenix, the year of its one Thousand nine hundred ninety-seventh civilized passing of the sun. One of each Thousand will endure, and as was intended, each shall govern themselves properly.

The Great Nation is indebted to many, far beyond her capability to repay. The Great Nation borrows on a promise of interest, repayment, favored status, and political control from one hand, and gives it freely to the other hand, without recourse. While her peoples suffer, the government of the Great Nation is buying control of other nations with trinkets it does not have; but the peoples have no control. Should the Great Nation discontinue its policy of supporting others, they will leave her and seek their welfare from others. The Great Nation is bankrupt and is held together by the purses of a downtrodden peoples.

The world is full of disease due to the fact that the peoples have placed their faith in scientific medicine rather than the Mother Earth for healing. Remember, there is nothing Mother Earth cannot cure as long is it comes from her; only manmade is man cured. Some of the manmade diseases of which I speak are AIDS, certain cancers (those of a chemically induced nature), drug dependency, alcohol dependency. Some would argue that man's medicines have advanced greatly and that cures must be near. Man knows those diseases he creates and their cures are in their uncreation. The reverse of what causes the disease holds the key to each cure.

Disease wrought by Mother Earth, such as cholesterol, high blood pressure, and afflictions of the skin and vital organs, can all be cured by turning to Mother Earth. Food intake alone will provide the health required to sustain the body. Food intake, which nourishes the body, also provides for the cleansing of the mind and spirit and is good for the soul and the god within.

The body rejects all that is considered waste to itself. Waste is excreted from the body through normal bodily outlets and functions—pores in the skin, the saliva, tears, blood, and hair.

The self-healing capabilities of the body are immense. The seeking of the inner soul to search out and rid the body of that which causes the disease or illness is without doubt the greatest medicine that exists. This ability was instilled in each by Mother Earth. Life and the body are a self-contained art. Self sustenance, self existence, self healing, of the One, for the One, by the One.

Many birth defects will not be remedied in modern times. Some birth defects are manmade, but many are organically correct. There is a reason for all that happens, including birth defects.

Drug dependency is a manmade disease. You will note

that the drugs that cause addiction are manmade. Most originated from derivatives obtained from Mother Earth, but many are now produced synthetically and for monetary gain. Man continually strives for ways and methods to make peoples dependent on each other. There is no unknown wisdom. The peoples can exist without the aid of others.

There is nothing more revered among the peoples of the world than the family unit, the ability and the desire to reproduce. It is sizeable and it is not. Remember, all are related to one another; all peoples are the same, having come from the same source.

Procreation is the way of Mother Earth and her peoples to sustain a working, self-sufficient population. Mother Earth has keyed her instructions into all peoples as to how many times they will reproduce, as well as how many times they will not.

An unsuccessful birth was not meant to be. We are not to grieve, nor are we to question why the birth was not meant to be. The peoples of the northern lands struggle with the question of procreation. While some religions demand procreation to sustain their memberships, others are lax and leave judgment in such matters to the bearer of the child.

When a woman chooses to abort a created child, she does so based upon the instructions she receives at her birthing from Mother Earth. Remember, no one peoples is here on Mother Earth that has not been upon a Mother Earth before. There are nearly 2,000 Mother Earths, so there is much room for rotation of the individual spirit. Remember, there is no death, only a changing of worlds. Original spirits never leave the plane upon which they reside. Floating spirits will share their experiences upon many Mother Earths.

Floating spirits are those who are destined to travel the Mother Earths and relive their past experiences upon each.

The knowledge amassed and the experiences shared unfold to create a blending of spirits that is more than one, but the same one. It is a guarantee that life originating from the One remains constant. A spirit more knowledgeable, more beautiful, more loving and more perfect than the original, we are now all that we were.

Mother Earth provides for herself all that she needs to survive. She has given of herself freely that her peoples shall endure. Her peoples, however, lack the wisdom of the future to understand that the path they have placed Mother Earth on is one of total destruction. Hindsight has been ignored and the peoples continue to take the fruits of Mother Earth for granted.

Many feel Mother Earth will last their own lifetime and that this is good enough. Many wonder why they should do anything to benefit those who will survive them. This in itself is a question that provides its own answer. All peoples will survive themselves. The changing of worlds will bring each back to this land once again and each will find that he was a purveyor of his own future suffering.

Building homes is a necessity Mother Earth agrees with. Homes may be built from any of the bounties Mother Earth provides. The construction of huge buildings, skyscrapers, as self-proclaimed importance to the skies is unnecessary. These buildings place unnecessary burdens upon Mother Earth.

Covering Mother Earth in concrete and asphalt is suffocating her. Pressure points within Mother Earth have been blocked and the retaliation will be deserved. The first children lived many generations upon Mother Earth without the ways of western civilization, and many still do so, if not physically, within their hearts.

The lands that were once plentiful for the innocent

ch:ldren, the animals, has been pillaged beyond regression. The innocent children, once plentiful, have been slaughtered and their numbers forcefully dwindled to make room for more unwarranted civilizations.

The plan for the animals was one of food. There were many and they produced in bounty for the survival of the peoples. More now are slaughtered for things other than food. They are slaughtered for adornments, clothing, trophies, and to vacate the land they inhabit. Once man has made the animals extinct, he will seek other means of satisfying his primal urges—each other, perhaps those less fortunate, those less perfect.

Unnecessary killing is yet another of man's ways of setting himself above all else. In one false breath man will say, "See me, I am civilized," and then, in a false act, will bear arms against the defenseless, innocent children. Killing is a primal instinct that failed to mature with man. Man will bear arms against anything or anyone, including himself.

There is no need for weapons of killing and destruction upon Mother Earth. The only purposes of such weapons are for superiority above all others and for killing one another. Military might shows man's cowardice and lack of conviction in himself. Military might is man's excuse for not following the plan of Mother Earth. Man does not have to learn to live in peace with one another as long as man has his weapons and his armies. Weapons and armies are of, and for, monetary gain.

For decades now, man has been planting the seeds of his filth deep in the bosom of Mother Earth. Nuclear waste and radioactive materials are buried deep within the Earth and the peoples are told this is good.

Man does not truly believe he is safe from their effects

once buried; he only hopes he is safe. That which was buried as recently as three to five years ago has already begun to rupture and fester, poisoning Mother Earth from below. The poison has already reached her waters and therefore, her peoples. The governments tell the peoples that all is well while the governments know that all is not well. The waters are the life of Mother Earth and all who live upon her. Killing the waters will result in killing the peoples.

Nuclear testing underground and in the waters is killing Mother Earth, who has already begun to gasp her last breath. The waters not only sustain Mother Earth, but all who live upon her. Kill the waters and you kill the peoples. Mother Earth will be the last to go; her departure will be lonely.

The chosen site for the destruction of nuclear weapons is a blanket of secrecy. Purportedly, the Johnson Atoll is the site where nuclear weapons will be destroyed and burned for the betterment of the peoples. The truth be known, many of the weapons are old and will not make the journey to the Atoll. Their poisons will be unleashed against the Pacific waters and within a short period of time, those waters, once laden with life, will lie dead. The governments have instilled regulations for the completion of these tasks, but the regulations are not enough and will be ignored by those too few in charge who will take it upon themselves to decide what is financially best.

The removal of the weapons of mass destruction from Mother Earth should be a global feat and those who provide for its accomplishment should do so without thought of monetary gain. Their best destruction is their slow discharge into the sun. This accomplishment will be without harm to the peoples.

The Grand Creation is perhaps the hardest reality for the peoples to accept. Life was not created without a reason, and the peoples would find it hard to believe that it was. Those *are the same peoples who cannot believe they were created in order to serve one God. This would be nothing less than slavery, they feel, so the question as to why the peoples are here and why Mother Earth exists has gone unanswered. Why is Mother Earth populated? Why are other Mother Earths, other planets populated? Would the planets not exist without human and/or animal life?*

To put these questions in perspective, we must remember the One. The One great planet if you will; one planet, more than 2,000 times the size of our Mother Earth, that once existed, then divided in accordance with the Grand Creation and gave of itself a gift of life to many.

Do not feel as if your own peoples are the only peoples who scoff the Grand Creation and its meaning, and who abuse their Mother Earth, because there are others who act likewise.

We have all been here before, we have all done this before, and our history of failures and achievements are buried within our Mother Earths. To seek the histories would be fruitless because we would not understand and will misinterpret that which we find.

We had walked nearly halfway down the mountainside during our conversations. I was amazed at Standing Wolf's wisdom and the obvious love he had for Mother Earth and her children. Never once did he raise his voice in anger, and some of the things he spoke of certainly could have made him do so.

This was the first time I had physically met the Indian man who entered my mind so many months ago; I wanted to talk to him forever. There was so much that I still wanted to know from him, and I wondered if I would be able to remember all that he had already shared with me this day.

Standing Wolf is the keeper of the cage of the Phoenix for those of us here on Earth. His spirit will never graduate to another world, as his assignment here is a permanent one.

Since I am his incarnate in this time, it saddens me to know that I will never spirit to another world either. From all that I have learned from this wise Indian man, there are countless numbers of hearts out among the stars that long to be touched, hands that long to be grasped in friendship, smiles that long to be shared.

Eternity is not such a long time, when you consider this type of wisdom is at your side. I am the Wolf, I know this now, and my assignment is the Mother Earth. She is my hope, my faith, and this glorious existence that she has given me shall not be wasted.

My soul was awakened just a short time ago. Here, on this mountain, my spirit was lifted and touched by the love of all that is in such a compassionate way. Sheer remembrance of it causes me to tremble. I am but a small bit of this, but I have been given a duteous task: the task of waking all of Mother Earth's children, the children of the world, to let them know that she is forever at our side, but she cries because we do not understand.

When we reached a clearing on the wooded mountainside, a woman was waiting to greet us. She was a small woman, which was about all I could tell from a distance. As we drew closer, I began to see her smile appear. Her long dark hair wafted lightly in the slow breeze. She wore a white robe emblazoned with painted blue symbols that I did not recognize. Her face, which I had seen but twice before, was now familiar; the sun glowed in its copper color. How had I not recognized her the second time we met? She was my helicopter pilot; she was Reeva. She reached her arms out to me as we approached and greeted me with a warm hug—exactly what I needed.

"You'll be needing this," she said, handing me an object. I opened my hand and into it she dropped the eye of the Wolf. "It will come in handy someday." She smiled.

I looked back at Standing Wolf, who had a look of proud approval on his face. His dark eyes confirmed his final words. "You will do well in the challenges to come," Standing Wolf said. His voice sounded not unlike a proud father watching his child's first step. "I have chosen you well, my son. Keep me forever in your heart, forever in your mind, for this is where I truly live." His voice had turned almost sullen. "I return you to your original place," he said, "and I grieve for the loss of your companionship. The love that was taken from you has been restored."

Standing Wolf placed the palm of his hands against my forehead; my eyes burned. He pushed slightly but not enough to make me lose my balance. I opened my eyes to the vision of the old Indian medicine man once more. He backed up several steps and nodded his head in a regal bow. Then slowly he turned and walked away, a white wolf, a new wolf at his side. He slowly faded, then disappeared into the woods. I felt empty, lost, and alone, except for Reeva, who was silent.

Reeva took my hand as I turned to begin my journey down the mountain. I took a single step and in an instant I was aboard my plane headed back to the United States. I looked around, startled, then calmed myself down. I was tired. I felt as if I hadn't slept in weeks and the truth was, I probably hadn't.

Mother Earth, the Healer

The following are some of the natural remedies Mother Earth provides for the health of her peoples. Most natural remedies listed below can be found in pure or derivative form in health-food stores. Note: an asterisk (*) denotes consumption warning; poison or narcotic effects.

Alfalfa (*Medicago sativa*): North America. Wild and agriculturally produced. Perhaps the best known natural blood purifier, it also has natural medicinal value to guard against hepatitis and arthritis. Consume in a strong tea or by the whole leaf.

Aloe (*Aquilaria*): Southwestern America, South Africa. Wild and agriculturally produced. Known to just about everyone, aloe is a remedy for sunburn, minor burns, skin abrasions and insect bites. Topical applications.

Angelica: Wild. The natural medicinal value of Angelica is its effects on the vital organs such as liver, lungs, and kidneys. It also guards against high blood pressure and hepatitis. Natural baked goods and teas.

Aspen (*Populus*): North America, tree, mainly in higher altitudes. Its bark is a medicine for colds, flu, and allergies. Aspen bark contains a natural mild antibiotic. Bark, stewed in teas.

Bitterroot (*Lewisia rediviva*): Western North America. Bitterroot contains a natural mild laxative. It is also effective in healing or deterring venereal disease, diabetes, worms, kidney stones, and gallstones.

Black Cohosh (*Caulophyllum thalictroides [Barberry]*):

115

North America. Remedy for high blood pressure, convulsions, rheumatism. Affects lungs and nervous system. Root, stewed in teas.

Black Hawthorn (*Crataegis*): North America, hedge, root/bark. Remedy for better blood circulation; guards against chills, fever, heart palpitations. Affects circulatory system, heart. Stewed in teas.

Boneset (*Eupatorium perfoliatum*): North America, plant. A bowel cleanser. Can be used to induce vomiting. Stewed in tea as a folk cold remedy.

Burdock (*Arctium*): North America, plant. Natural ingredients act as a blood purifier and guard against pleurisy. This root contains a natural cancer deterrent. Stewed in teas or brewed with coffee.

Capsicum: North America, fruit, red pepper. Natural healing aide deterrent for ear infections, pneumonia, chills, sinusitis. Improves blood circulation, acts as blood builder. Acts on blood and blood vessels. Stewed in teas.

Celery (*Apium graveolens*): North America. Vegetable. Raw or celery tea. Acts as a blood cleanser; works on liver, spleen. Effective against hepatitis, tonsillitis, insomnia, arthritis.

Chamomile (*Anthemis nobilis and Matricaria*): North America. Most widely known as tea. Remedy for jaundice, liver and spleen ailments. Natural deodorant. Further used for anemia, appendicitis pain, gall bladder afflictions, colic, infant convulsions, measles, and as a diuretic. Leaf, stewed in teas.

Chaparral Pea (*Pickeringia montana*): Southwest United States. Shrub. Acts against hepatitis; dissolves cancer tumors; remedies arthritis; is a blood purifier and diuretic. Stewed in teas.

Chicory (*Cichorium intybus*): North America, plant. Acts against hepatitis, tonsillitis, anemia, appendicitis; remedy for liver and spleen disorders. Leaf stewed in teas. Root roasted in coffee.

Chokecherry (*Prunus virginiana*): North America, Tree. Remedy for lung congestion, colds, flu, cough. Stewed in teas. Smoked for headache, dizziness. Compress for ulcerated wounds, and as topical antibiotic.

Cinquefoil (*Potentilla*): North America, flower. Remedy for abdominal cramps, appendicitis; internal pain reliever. Stewed in teas. Mashed into a paste for rashes, sores, bruises, and sprains.

Coltsfoot (*Tussilage farfara*): North America, plant. Remedy for bronchitis, whooping cough, sinusitis, asthma. Stewed in teas, leaf raw in salad.

Comfrey (*Symphytum*): North America, water plant. A pain reliever; acts against internal hemorrhaging and as an antitoxin. Stewed in teas. As a mashed compress for burns, ulcerated wounds, oral ulcerations, sore throats, boils, arthritis.

Cowslip(*) (*Primula veris*): North America, shrub. Remedy for warts, skin lesions, tumors, rash. Sap from shrub used in drops.

Cucumber Root (*Cucumis sativus*): North America, gourd/plant. Acts against scurvy, dandruff, lice. Ingest wild greens in salad.

Dandelion (*Dentis taraxacum*): North America, Global, weed. Acts against hives, cancer, malignant skin lesions, acne, warts. An antiseptic and blood cleanser. Ingest leaf in salads. Boiled root tea for rheumatism, liver and spleen disorders, headache, hepatitis, appendicitis, and as a blood builder.

Echinacea (*Echinacea purpurea [Central U.S.]*) (*Echinacea angustifolia [North America]*): Herb. Remedy for burns, wounds, boils, skin cancers, lesions, and ear infections. Root, either raw or boiled as a wash. Stewed in tea for a strong blood filter, antitoxin, and remedy for sinusitis, ulcers, pneumonia.

Elderberry(*) (*Sambucus*): North America, shrub. Acts against ulcers, blisters, burns, skin fungus. Use in raw or mashed compress. Berries ward off vitamin and mineral deficiency; use as diuretic.

Elecampane (*Inula helenium*): North America, plant. Acts against muscle pain, back pain, toothache, worms, pulmonary ailments, cough, alcoholism. Stewed in teas.

Eucalyptus: North America, tree. Active against asthma, bronchitis, tumors, ulcers, worms, pleurisy, sore throats, and sinusitis. Stewed in teas.

Feverwort (*Triosteum perfoliatum*): North America, bush. Remedy for coughs, fever, jaundice, gangrene, tonsillitis, hepatitis. Stewed in teas, ingest fruit.

Fireweed (*Epilobium angustifolium*): North America, herb. Remedy for hay fever, diarrhea, and tonsillitis, stewed in tea. Acts against scurvy and anemia; boiled wild greens. Root raw/mashed as compress for swelling and leg pains.

Flatspine Ragweed(*) (*Ambrosia elatior*): North America, weed. Stewed in tea to promote menstruation and assist in contraception.

Ginseng (*Panax quinquefolius*): North America, ivy/plant. Acts against cough, exhaustion. Use as blood builder, sexual stimulant, memory improver. Raw root ingested as digestive aid, prostate aid; helps to retard or slow cancer growths. Remedy for menstrual cramps. Combats natural radiation effects in the body. Stewed in teas.

Golden Ragwort(*) (*Senecio aureus*): North America, plant. Antidote for poison under skin, eases childbirth, and aids contraception. Stewed in teas.

Goldenseal(*) (*Hydrastis canadensis*): North America, plant. Remedy for wounds, eczema, boils, gum lesions, skin cancers, toothache, oral lesions, hemorrhoids; mashed into a paste. Stewed in teas for prostate ailments, asthma, cancers, jaundice, colitis, ulcers, diabetes. A blood builder and purifier, remedy for bladder and abdominal ailments, alcoholism.

Strong compositions of the plant, when prepared as a thick douche, can produce self-induced abortion.

Gooseberry (*Ribes*): North America, shrub. Remedy for kidney stones, fever, chills. Stew in teas or ingest raw fruit.

Henbane(*) (*Hyoscyamus niger*): North America, plant. Acts against swellings as a bathing additive. Dried and smoked as a hypnotic, hallucinogen. Stewed in weak tea for coughs, insomnia, gall bladder ailments, and allergies. Acts as sedative.

Hops (*Hunulus americanus*): North America, vine. Active as sedative, remedy for coughs, insomnia, allergies, gall bladder ailments, jaundice, and liver ailments. Stewed in teas. Mashed as salve for itching skin, rashes, skin lesions, and hives.

Horehound (*Marrubium vulgare*): North America, plant. Remedy for coughs, pulmonary ailments, jaundice, asthma, hoarseness. Used as a laxative; remedy for chills, worms, tonsillitis, and diabetes. Stewed in teas.

Horsetail (*Equisetum*): North America, plant. Acts against diabetes, kidney ailments, appendicitis. Use as diuretic stewed in teas. As a mashed compress for gangrene, ulcerated wounds, and burns.

Indian [North American] Hemp(*) (*Apocynum cannarbium*): North America, plant/weed. When mashed as a poultice, a remedy for hemorrhoids, sties. Ground into a paste for ulcerated sores; dissolves skin lesions. Stewed in tea for kidney ailments, heart stimulant, antidepressant, blood circulation, asthma, and exhaustion.

Indian Lettuce (*Pyrola americana*): North America, plant. Acts against scurvy and anemia. Raw leaf ingested in salad.

Jimsonweed(*) (*Datura stramonium*): North America, weed. Leaves dried and smoked produce hypnotic sedative/hallucinogen. Acts against asthma. Use mashed as a compress for bruises, swellings, sprains, spider and rattlesnake bites.

Juniper (*Juniperus*): North America, shrub. As a mashed

119

compress for burns, as an antiseptic, acne, athlete's foot, dandruff. As a paste for external hemorrhaging.

Lady's Slipper (*Cypripedium*): North America, flower/orchid. Acts against pain, headache, as a sedative, as a tranquilizer for insomnia. Stewed in teas.

Larkspur(*) (*Delphinium*): North America, herb. The root, when boiled, is used for head and body lice.

Lichen (*Alga and Fungus*): North America, moss. Stewed in teas for colds, pleurisy, bronchitis.

Lobelia(*) (*Lobeliaceae*): North America, herb. Remedy for hepatitis, spasms, colic, venereal disease, colitis, coughs, bronchitis, convulsions, pleurisy, arthritis, and bladder disorders. Stewed in teas. As a hypnotic, insomnia, and headache deterrent. Mashed into a compress for hemorrhoids, skin cancer; draws out boils/skin lesions.

Magnolia (*Magnoliaceae*): North America, flowering shrub/tree. Boiled into an oil wash for dandruff. Stewed in teas for rheumatism, fever, chills, and aching joints.

Maize (*Zea mays*): North America, plant [corn]. The silk is stewed into teas for bed wetting, high blood pressure, and as a liver stimulant.

Mandrake(*) (*Podophyllum peltatum*): North America, tree [mayapple]. The root is stewed in teas for bladder incontinence, liver ailments, asthma, poor blood circulation, insomnia, worms, and as a poison antidote. The resin paste is used against warts, tumors and skin cancers.

Mescal Bean(*) (*Sophora secundiflora*): Southwest North America, shrub. The raw bean chewed is a euphoric hallucinogen.

Mistletoe (*Phoradendron and viscun*): North America, plant/parasite. The leaf, stewed in teas, induces labor.

Mountain Ash (*Sorbus americana*): North America, tree. Active against hepatitis and allergies. As an antiseptic and blood purifier. Bark, stewed in teas. The berry, ingested raw, deters scurvy.

Mullein (*Verbascum*): North America, plant. The flower, stewed in teas, acts as a pain reliever for headache, and as a blood purifier, balances acid in the system, and as an antitoxin for cancer. Effective against acne. Acts against liver and spleen disorders, swollen glands, and hepatitis. The leaf, mashed into a compress, acts against tonsillitis, ulcers, skin cancers, acne, and warts. As a poultice for back pain.

Nettle (*Urtica*): North America, plant. Acts against fever, bronchitis, scurvy, tonsillitis, jaundice, liver ailments, prostate ailments, hepatitis. As a diuretic. Stewed in teas. As a mashed compress for rheumatism, neuralgia, and arthritis.

Oak (*Quercus*): North America, tree/shrub. Acts against diarrhea and appendicitis. Bark stewed in teas. Mold of the acorn raw as a compress, for wounds as an antibiotic, against ticks and conjunctivitis. The inner bark, boiled, as a gargle/douche against tonsillitis, vaginal infections.

Palma Christi (*Ricinus communis*): North America, plant. A natural castor oil plant. Mashed into a compress for internal ailments, tumors, hepatitis. Boiled compress for boils, swellings, sprains, sore throats, ulcers. Boiled as a wash for use as insect repellent. Crushed into a liniment for skin blemishes, chapped skin, skin lesions, and tumors.

Parsley (*Petroselinum*): North America, plant. Acts against kidney stones, heart palpitations, poor blood circulation, and gallstones. Blood builder and a potassium/vitamin B source. Leaf stewed in teas. Mashed into a compress for swollen glands, insect bites and stings. Root, stewed in teas for jaundice, liver and spleen disorders, high blood pressure, arthritis, hepatitis, and as a diuretic.

Pasture Brake (*Pteridium polypodiaceae*): North America, plant/fern. Acts against flatulence, diarrhea, indigestion, menstrual cramps. Use as a skin softener. Root stewed in teas.

Pennyroyal (*Mentha pulegium*): North America, plant/mint. Acts against scurvy, flatulence, chills; relieves abdominal cramps, colic; promotes menstruation and aids contraception. Leaf stewed in teas. Leaf, raw, ingested as breath freshener.

Peyote(*) (*Lophophora williamsi*): North America, plant/cactus. Acts like mescaline, a strong hallucinogen. Dried and chewed/ingested.

Pine (*Pinus*): North America, tree. Bark, mashed into a compress, acts as burn antibiotic. Inner bark, mashed into a compress, acts against pleurisy, used for ulcerated wounds, boils and acne. The sap, boiled as a wash, used for antiseptic, deodorant, acne, and dandruff. Nuts, roasted and ground, are a remedy for vitamin deficiency. The needles are stewed in teas for scurvy, ulcers, venereal disease, and anemia.

Pipsissewa (*Chimaphila umbellata*): North America, bush/heath. Acts against diabetes and bladder disorders, eases childbirth. Leaf stewed in teas. Root mashed into a compress for swollen glands, ulcers, tonsillitis, blisters, and skin lesions.

Plantain (*Plantago*): North America, weed. Leaf mashed into a compress for cuts and abrasions. Leaf boiled and crushed into a paste for blisters, infection, boils, and cracked lips. Leaf stewed in teas for worms and slowing of menstrual flow. Leaf crushed into a wash for rattlesnake bite, poisonous insect antidote, eczema, burns, ulcerated wounds, and cracked lips. Seed stewed in teas for laxative, ulcers, hepatitis, liver ailments, tonsillitis, and swollen glands. Root mashed into a poultice for toothaches.

Pleurisy Root (*Asclepias tuberosa*): North America, milkweed. Leaf stewed in teas acts as expectorant, for fever, inducing vomiting, chest pains, and chills. Root stewed in teas for flatulence. Root, roasted and ingested, for bronchitis, pleurisy, and asthma. Root mashed into paste for minor wounds. Sap made into paste for warts.

Pokeroot(*) (*Phytolacca*): North America, herb [Poke-weed, Pokeberry]. Shoots wild greens, boiled for vitamin deficiency and anemia. Root stewed in teas for asthma, bronchitis, ulcers, swollen glands, ringworm, tumors, warts, spleen disorders, heart palpitations, high blood pressure, hepatitis, and appendicitis. The berry, mashed into a paste, acts against skin cancers, ear infections, boils, ulcerated wounds, swelling, warts, acne, and as an antitoxin.

Prickly Pear (*Opuntia*): Northeast United States, plant/cactus. Active against infected sores, appendicitis, spider bites, pulp, boiled into a compress. Stems mashed into compress for ulcerated wounds, warts, and skin lesions.

Puffball (*Fungi*): North America, Global, plant. Remedy for minor wounds, burns, external infections and bleeding; also an antibiotic. Dried and powdered.

Purslane (*Portulaca*): North America, Global, herb. Active against vitamin deficiency, anemia; chewed and ingested. Boiled as a wash for fever, skin inflammations, hives, itching, and rashes. Juice of the stem used as a gargle for cough, bronchitis, lung congestion. Seed stewed in teas for insomnia, worms, and as a sexual stimulant.

Red Clover (*Trifolium pratense*): North America, Global, plant/legume. The flower, stewed in teas acts against liver ailments, gall bladder ailments, ulcers. As a blood purifier, antitoxin. Acts against hepatitis, diabetes, tonsillitis, or as a throat gargle, against internal cancer, appendicitis, as a bowel cleanser, for headache, and as a sedative. The flower crushed as a salve for ulcerated wounds, tumors, boils, skin cancer, and liver spots. The leaf chewed and ingested for scurvy and as an appetite enhancer. The leaf boiled into a compress against abscesses, burns, boils, skin cancer, liver spots, and freckles.

Redroot (*Ceanothus and Lacnanthes tinctoria*): North America, Atlantic coast, shrub [Pigweed]. Leaf stewed in teas for sore throat. Root stewed in teas to use as sedative, for headache, joint pain, muscle aches, and convulsions.

Sage (*Salvia*): North America, Global, herb. Stewed in teas. Used for upset stomach, nausea, flatulence, liver ailments, kidney and gallstones, gargle for mouth and gum lesions, swollen glands, tonsillitis, hepatitis, and as an antidepressant. Juice of the leaf in drops used for warts, skin cancers, and tumors.

Salisfy (*Tragopogon pornifolius*): North America, Global, root [Oyster Plant]. Sap stewed in teas for gallstones.

Sarsaparilla (*Aralia nudicaulis*): Eastern North America, shrub. Root stewed in teas for venereal disease, appendicitis, and as a blood purifier. Root mashed into a compress for infections and as an antidote for poisons.

Sassafras (*Sassafra albidum*): Eastern North America, tree. Flower stewed in teas for fevers, chills, congestion, and constipation. Leaf crushed into a compress for skin lesions, wounds, hives. Bark mashed into a compress for sore eyes and ear infections. Root mashed into a compress to remedy bruises, sprains, and swelling. Root bark stewed in teas for kidney ailments, high blood pressure, bronchitis, and as a bowel cleanser. Promotes heavy perspiration.

Saxifrage (*Saxifragaceae*): North America [temperate], plant. Leaf stewed in teas to remedy kidney and bladder ailments. Leaf as a wild green in salads for anemia and scurvy.

Scurvy Grass (*Cochlearia officinalis*): North America, Arctic, plant [mustard]. Leaf and stem as wild greens used for scurvy and anemia.

Serviceberry (*Amelanchier*): North America, tree, shrub [Juneberry]. Inner bark boiled as a wash for sore eyes. Young berries stewed in tea for diarrhea. Mature berry mashed and ingested for scurvy and anemia.

Shepherd's Purse (*Capsella Bursa-pastoris*): North America, weed [mustard]. Leaf crushed as a compress to remedy minor wounds, bruises, and ear infections. Stewed in teas for internal hemorrhaging and ulcers. Leaf raw as wild greens for scurvy. Pod roasted for vitamin deficiency and anemia. Sap soaked in moss as a compress for nosebleeds.

Skullcap (*Scutellaria*): North America, plant/mint. Acts as a sedative; remedy for headaches, fever, cramps, insomnia, high blood pressure, heart palpitations, allergies, coughs. Leaf stewed in teas.

Slippery Elm (*Ulmus rubra*): North America, tree. Inner bark mashed into a paste to remedy ulcerated wounds, boils, skin cancer, minor burns. Inner bark stewed in teas as a laxative, antitoxin, and to remedy bursitis. Inner bark boiled as a wash for chapped skin, rashes, and skin lesions. Root stewed in tea for ulcers. Eases childbirth.

Solomon's Seal (*Polygonatum*): North America, flower/lily. Root boiled as a wash for freckles, liver spots, bruises, and hemorrhaging wounds.

Sorrel (*Oxydendrum arboreum*): North America, tree [sourwood]. Leaf stewed in teas for stomach hemorrhaging. Leaf as wild greens used for anemia and scurvy. Leaf crushed into a compress for skin lesions, boils, and warts. Root stewed in teas slows menstrual flow and nosebleeds.

Spleenwort Fern (*Asplenium*): South West United States, plant/fern. Leaf stewed in teas to remedy abdominal cramps, diarrhea; eases childbirth and spleen disorders. Leaf boiled as a wash for blisters, poison ivy, skin abrasions/lesions, insect bites, and ear infections.

Squawberry (*Mitchella repens*): Eastern North America, herb [Partridgeberry, Twinberry, Teaberry]. Berry ingested raw for diarrhea. Leaf stewed in teas for bleeding, and to prevent miscarriage. Reduces menstrual flow and discomfort.

Starwort (*Stellaria*): North America, flower/aster. Leaf crushed into a compress to remedy swelling, abscesses, boils, ulcerated wounds, infected sores, and hemorrhoids. Leaf stewed in teas for cancer, constipation, hepatitis, swollen glands, tonsillitis, appendicitis, and as a blood purifier. Leaf raw as wild greens for vitamin deficiency and anemia.

Stonecrop (*Sedum*): North America, perennial. Leaf crushed into a poultice for warts, skin tumors, skin cancer, and gangrene. Leaf stewed in teas for moderate fever, ulcers, kidney stones, and appendicitis. Leaf crushed as a juice wash to remedy ulcerated sores and boils.

Sumac (*) (*Rhus/(*)Toxico dendron*): North America, nut plant/cashew. Flower boiled as a wash for sore and infected eyes and sties. Bark boiled as a wash for burns, sunburn, eczema, psoriasis, blisters, external bleeding, hives, itching, and rashes. Inner bark boiled as a wash for an astringent. Sap as a paste for toothache. Juice as a salve for infected sores and wounds. Berry boiled as a gargle for sore throat and oral lesions. Root stewed in teas for internal hemorrhaging and ulcers.

Sunflower (*Helianthus*): North America. Flower boiled as a wash to remedy arthritis, rheumatism, and bursitis. Seed ingested raw for bronchitis, scurvy, chills; promotes perspiration. Seed stewed in teas as a prostate rejuvenator and diuretic. Root mashed into a compress for bruises, blisters, snake bites, spider bites.

Tansy (*) (*Senecio jacobaea*): North America, plant. Whole leaf stewed in teas as a contraceptive. Flower stewed in teas to remedy fever, gall bladder ailments, worms, and heart palpitations. Leaf boiled as a wash for lower leg and joint pains. Leaf crushed into a compress for minor sprains and headache. Seeds stewed in teas as a laxative; promotes menstruation. Seed mashed into a compress for bruises, sunburn, warts, freckles, back pain, skin growths, and cancer tumors. Sap boiled as a wash to use as insect repellent.

Thyme (*Thymus*): North America, Global, herb/mint. Leaf crushed into a compress as an antiseptic and for cankers. Leaf

126

stewed in teas for colic, flatulence, colds, bronchitis, whooping cough; promotes heavy perspiration. Leaf crushed into a liniment to remedy neuralgia, arthritis, rheumatism, toothache, swelling, pain, and as a deodorant.

Uva-Ursi [Kinnikinnick] (*Arctostaphylos*): North America, heath/bush [Bearberry]. Leaf stewed in teas for hepatitis, internal hemorrhaging, acne, and as a blood purifier. Berry ingested raw as a diuretic; for prostate ailments, diabetes, and kidney stones.

Valerian (*Velerian officanilas*): North America, northern hemisphere, herb. Root stewed in teas as a sedative and for abdominal cramps, headache, heart palpitations, insomnia, hypertension, anemia, and convulsions.

Walnut (*Juglans/Juglandacae*): North America, northern hemisphere, tree. Leaf boiled as a wash for eczema, hives, boils, ulcerated sores, as an astringent, and external hemorrhaging. Bark boiled as a wash for arthritis, skin lesions, chicken pox, measles, and itching rashes. Inner bark stewed in teas as a laxative, for ulcers, and diverticulitis. Hulls mashed in a syrup for worms. Hull juice used as a wash for head and body lice, and dandruff. Nut ingested raw for vitamin deficiency and anemia.

Watercress (*Nasturtium officinale*): North America, plant. Leaf as wild greens for acidity balance; high in vitamin E. Leaf stewed in teas for liver ailments, stamina, hepatitis, tonsillitis, swollen glands, kidney stones, spleen pain, acidity balancer, aging, anemia, and as a sedative and heart strengthener.

White Pond Lily (*Nelumbium pentapetalum*): North America, plant/lotus. Root stewed in teas to remedy bladder ailments, diarrhea, prostate ailments, kidney ailments. Root mashed as a poultice for oral lesions and tooth pain.

Wild Lettuce (*Lactuca canadensis*): Eastern North America, weed [dandelion]. Juice/syrup as a pain reliever, for headaches, intestinal calmative, abdominal cramps, and as a hypnotic sedative. Sap boiled as a paste for hives, toothache, poison ivy, and poison oak. Sap boiled as a syrup against bronchitis and coughs.

Wild Rice (*Zizania aquatica*): North America, grass/weed. Rice, boiled or raw for high blood pressure and heart palpitations.

Willow (*Salix*): North America, shrub/tree. Leaf mashed into a poultice to remedy nosebleeds, toothache, and hemorrhoids. Bark as a wash for astringent, detergent, dandruff. Inner bark stewed in teas for venereal disease. Inner bark mashed into a compress for infections, wounds, gangrene, bleeding, and as an antibiotic.

Wintergreen (*Gaultheria procumbens*): North America, shrub/evergreen. Leaf boiled as a gargle for sore throats. Leaf mashed into a compress to remedy swelling, sore muscles, joint pain, pleurisy, and sprains. Leaf stewed in teas for ulcers, colic, gall bladder disorders, internal hemorrhaging, liver and spleen disorders and flatulence. Berries ingested raw promote breast milk flow.

Witch Hazel (*Hamamelis virginina*): Eastern North America, shrub. Whole boiled for steam for bronchitis, flu, and coughs. Leaf crushed into a compress for swellings, bruises, and sprains. Leaf boiled in teas for stomach ulcers and external hemorrhaging.

Wormwood (*Artemisia*): North America, plant. Leaf stewed in teas to remedy emphysema, bladder disorders, worms, jaundice, tonsillitis, liver and spleen disorders, colitis, hepatitis, appendicitis, and as a blood purifier. Leaf crushed into a liniment for sprains, bruises, swellings, rheumatism, arthritis, bursitis, and back pain.

Yarrow(*) (*Achillea millefolium*): North America, plant. Leaf mashed as a poultice for toothache, oral lesions, and ear infections. Leaf mashed into a compress as an anesthetic and to remedy external hemorrhaging. Leaf boiled as a wash for an anesthetic, burns, sore muscles, irritated eyes, measles, chicken pox, hives, poison ivy, and poison oak. Root stewed in teas for internal hemorrhaging, colds, swollen glands, hepatitis, gall bladder disorders, diabetes, as a blood purifier and appetite enhancer. Root stewed in strong teas as a contraceptive.

Yellow Dock (*Rumex*): North America, weed [Buckwheat]. Leaf as wild greens remedies scurvy. High in vitamins A and C. Root stewed in teas for ulcers, swollen glands, tonsillitis, hepatitis, liver and spleen disorders, anemia, coughing, and as a blood builder. Root mashed into a compress for swellings, ulcerated wounds, cysts, and joint pains.

Yerba Santa (*Micromeria chamissonis*): Pacific North America, plant/mint, evergreen. Leaf mashed as a compress to remedy rheumatism, skin pains, hemorrhoids, hives, skin lesions, and swelling. Leaf dried and smoked for asthma, bronchitis, and lung congestion. Leaf stewed in teas to induce vomiting, to remedy diarrhea, coughs, ulcers and bronchitis.

Yucca (*Yucca*): North America, agave/plant. Leaf stewed in teas for arthritis, fever, headache, rheumatism, ulcers, and appendicitis. Fruit ingested raw as a laxative. Root mashed into a compress for ulcerated wounds and sores, hives, chicken pox, itching, rashes, and gangrene.

NOTE: These natural remedies are not meant to replace medications, treatments, or therapies currently used by readers. They are for reference only. Natural remedies listed as having contraceptive effects are not guaranteed and should not replace current contraceptive measures, if any, being used by readers.

Night Journeys

During my dreams, I was literally treated to night travels. I met many people, some interesting, some bitter; all were from the past except one, who was from the future.

Each had something to share, something to teach, something to offer. Even those who were bitter toward me offered a lesson in what they, in bitterness, had to say.

I have given much thought to the "why" question here. These journeys were a genuine treat, but I lacked a reason for why I was traveling. I knew there was much to learn and there were many who were willing to teach. Even more puzzling was my uncanny ability to recall, verbatim, what everyone had to say.

These travels were not just visual but physical as well. I had deep feelings during them. My five senses were fully operative; I could see, hear, touch, taste, and smell everything. I felt the touch of a hand, the brushing of a tree branch, the smell of an encampment, or food in preparation. I could smell flowers and taste the pure waters. I felt genuine joy in meeting a new person and sensed his or her joy in meeting me. There were times in my travels when my clothing and appearance were my own; there were times when it was not, but I was clothed to fit in with the time and place.

I have learned that many refer to these journeys as *astral travel*. If that is what it is called, then call it such. The only journey I can relate to as astral travel was the first set of dreams that kept repeating themselves.

For those of you who have yet to figure out what the

reoccurring dream was suggesting, I can now tell you what it was. The expanding and contracting nebula I encountered represented my lungs and the black marks within the nebula represented the growths that were found on my lungs during an annual physical examination. I had the problem taken care of and it was eradicated from my body.

When Standing Wolf referred to taking my hand in the Valley of the Sun, he was referring to Arizona, where I had the problem treated. Standing Wolf came to me during the procedure, while I was under anesthesia, and took my hand. During this "dream," he also passed the blue feather through my throat and it emerged completely white except for a few black streaks. I still have this feather today and the black streaks have since disappeared. This affliction of the lungs was obviously something that could have taken my life, and I would not be here today to relate these stories had Standing Wolf not taken my hand in the Valley of the Sun (or anywhere else). This is one kick-ass Indian, let me be blunt. I don't know anyone who has received the favors I have. It bothers me to realize that not everyone can have the same experiences that I have had.

If nothing else in return, I have shared with Standing Wolf my never-ending wit and keen sense of humor. There were times when I would try a crack right to his face—and nothing! Not so much as a twitch. But as I neared the end of my time with Standing Wolf—what he called his "Shine Time"—I am pleased to report that I was able to hear and to share his great boisterous laughter. Once I understood all that he wished to share with me, Standing Wolf was able to come down to my level and enjoy the fruits of life I had to offer. While I do not believe that life should be full of laughs and a carefree attitude, I insist that everyone try it because it has always been a great help to me. Once you have a sense of humor, you can grasp the realities of life with better understanding.

On a not-so-funny note, I feel that in all fairness I should inform you that now that my task appears to be complete with these writings, the afflictions of my lungs have returned, as well as other ailments that are equally serious to me. I feel that since I am only to share a short five more years on this Mother Earth, they are destined to be the mother of all battles for me, which is perhaps how it should be.

Never go out with a whine, go out with a mighty whoop! A gift as priceless as life itself should never be released without a fight. I don't know who we have to prove it to, but I believe we must justify to someone that our gift of life was received with great appreciation. Validation of your life begins at birth and does not end until the final arrow has been drawn.

The Wolf is no longer constantly at my side and I have no one taking my hand. This will be the final test. I will either prove that I am worthy of the rebirth to come or I will disappear into the thoughts and memories of others. Either way I am convinced that I have made a mark, am making a mark, and will continue to make a mark as others after me validate their own lives.

A personal note to those I will eventually leave behind: I want jokes, laughter, and revelry at my passing because those of you who truly know me well know that this is how I lived my life.

To those readers who wonder how such beauty like that contained in these writings can come from a self-proclaimed smart ass like me: let your wonderment give credence to the fact that everything in these pages was given to me. Standing Wolf is out there and he has quite a chore ahead of him. I don't know if I was his first or if I'm his last One, but I'm glad that I'm in there somewhere and that he touched me.

Now I would like to share the thoughts and words of others as they were shared with me during my night journeys.

Bitter Cloud: My visit with Bitter Cloud was personal and physical. She was very kind and treated me almost as someone who had been injured. She was careful in her words, and an obvious concern for me was constantly worn on her face. She spoke somewhat slowly:

Destiny can be a wonderful thing, as long as we are prepared for the destiny we have created and do not allow ourselves to be shaken by the unfolding results, good or bad. This is one of the main ways Native Americans have endured. Though we know our destiny is chosen, along with good must come bad. It is fruitless to try to change one's destiny once it begins to unfold; it is a sensitive and carefully laid out plan.

The Bible tells of a race of peoples who suffered in bondage at the hands of the Pharaohs of Egypt. You would think that this suffering would be with purpose, but questions rise. The story tells of their deliverance from their bondage by the god they worshiped, only to be shunned by their god and cast out of his graces for forty years, simply for a momentary loss of faith. A true god would not do such things. Faith in themselves, their own inner spirit, their inner god—these are what truly brought them out of bondage, and is that which cast them back into it. The freedoms earned caused the swelling of heads that led them into decadence.

Of all the tribes and all the nations, there are those who hold fast to the morals and ideals of the old ways. The simple life was enough for many of us. Other races envisioned a different future for the native peoples. A more limited, controlled future, and one to be lived in a much smaller environment than we were accustomed to.

Was it wrong that the peoples lived a simple life, one of tribes, camps, and families? Not only do I not think so, but it sickens my heart that I should even have to ask myself this. I know that my peoples lived in peace within the family, giving support to one another freely. I know that my peoples did their best to be one with Mother Earth and to live upon her without greed. To preserve all that she was and to make every effort to leave her a better place for the young ones to inherit.

Other races came with weapons of great killing. Guns and more guns. They killed freely. Not only my peoples, but the animals. They destroyed the lands and the life of the lands and ravaged for the sake of their own greed. They wished to take our lands and our animals. When they could not defeat us, they made treaties with us and sent us to smaller lands. White man envisioned progress, envisioned a bigger, better place to inhabit. Look what they have done to my Mother Earth. Of course I have a heavy heart; of course I am angry; they are murdering my Mother Earth.

She understands what is being done to her, but her only method of fighting back is to take away all that she has given. All races will die, and Mother Earth will sleep in sickened peace. When she awakens, the new gifts she will have to offer will only be enjoyed by those most deserving, and I do not believe the white man will be among them.

Why do you suppose the symbol of your journey is the White Wolf? Why do you suppose the chosen for your task is a white man? Why do you think the tribes greet you with open arms? Knew they your father? Probably not. Knew they your brothers? Possibly. Know they your purpose and convictions? Definitely. This is a suffering in itself. You are strong willed, yes, but your spirit, it is that which is being challenged. Do you believe? You are not being made to feel the transgressions of your white brothers, for they are not your brothers.

It was said that the Red Nation would send forth its spirits into the white man, then task him to tell the story, task him to send the message. He would be challenged to face his greatest fears and he would be brought to know the illness to come. The knowledge will not be spread to prevent the illness; it is too late. The knowledge will be spread so that all will know why it is happening and that their ending will not be peaceful. Let them all dread the final day and look forward to it with heavy hearts. Let them not have the peaceful existence they took from others. Let them tremble.

My thoughts are with you as you journey. I am Bitter Cloud, One of each Thousand, true daughter of the Mother Earth.

Proud Mountain: A young warrior who was not a warrior. His is a time when warriors are not needed. His task was to guide me through the near future, provide a vision of a Mother Earth yet to come. He *never* took his hand off my shoulder. He always looked to me for a question after all that he had shown me. I had none. I did not need to question what I saw because I knew all too well what it was:

If the future of mankind depended solely on his own abilities, mankind would have ceased to exist long ago. Man refuses to recognize the power of Mother Earth. Man refuses to recognize the power behind the Grand Creation. Man cannot do all that he has done alone, but he refuses to believe this.

When Mother Earth begins to shed her lands and displace them with water, man will see it coming. In fact, man will have much warning. Man will try to hold back the waters. Walls will be built, dikes set in place—all to no avail. Mother Earth is going to reclaim herself; she is going to rid herself of her unworthy children. Let this sound as cruel to you as it will. There is truly nothing more cruel than that which the children of Mother Earth have done to her.

The rising of the waters has already begun. Smaller floods throughout North America and worldwide. Man has thus far coped with the damage, which is minimal compared to what it will be. The sun is warming Mother Earth and her frozen tears have begun to weep. The damage to Mother Earth's natural shield is disastrously worse than the peoples have been led to believe. There are those who have tried to warn the peoples, but they have been silenced.

The word has been sent out to all Mother Earths: "Send your children here no more, this Mother Earth is dying." And the other worlds will listen. The other existing Mother Earths, they will instill in their children the desire to seek other than this planet as they journey and transcend the spiritual plain. When this Mother Earth is ready, she will call for the return of the One of each Thousand. She will call them home once more and she will be a beautiful, bountiful, caring Mother Earth again.

The One of each Thousand that you have seen in your journeys will have the new knowledge and wisdom instilled that they may live the land once more. Mother Earth will not let her children poison her again; she will return them lacking the desire to do this.

Since the beginning, many of the Mother Earths have died. They have spread their spirits out among their sisters for safekeeping and their sisters welcomed them with all they had to give. The children were appreciative. These children were sent with the knowledge of what they had done to their own Mother Earth and their spirit, lost in the blending of their new families, spoke out in an attempt to right the wrongs on this Mother Earth before the damage was done. I sometimes fear that they were too late, but they were not.

When the One of each Thousand of this Mother Earth spirits, they will be welcomed home by the Lojon. They will be cared for, nurtured, educated, and loved. They will prepare for their return to a land much less than that which they departed.

When Mother Earth finishes her healing, the lands that will be left will be less than North America has now. It will be one land instead of many set apart from one another as they are now. Those most deserving, the One of each Thousand, will enjoy the land and appreciate that which will have been given to them once more. They will live the land together in peace and in family. The waters will be pure again and their bounties will be many. Those children who had become extinct will return so that all who once lived apart will live an eternity in love.

Shed not a tear for this future, for it is truly necessary. Shed not a tear for this future, for it is beautiful. Shed not a tear for this future, for it is yours. An innocent man will lead them; they will love him and he will love them back. He will carry the wisdom, and unlike those of today, he will share the wisdom with all of his brothers and sisters. They will know of the Mother Earth past. They will keep this memory in disgust and they will keep it from happening again.

All will be one tribe, all will be one family, all will love one another. As always, there will be no death, only a changing of worlds.

I am Proud Mountain, One of each Thousand, true son of the Mother Earth.

Red Hawk in Winter: If there were a description of the modern Native American woman, Red Hawk is all that one would be. Her tongue was modern and her comments sometimes flippant, yet to the point; in fact she was downright bitchy! A very bitter woman, Red Hawk was not completely sure of the role she was to play in my journeys. I concluded that hers was to keep me from getting too big for my britches and to make me realize that what I was experiencing was truly special:

The last time I dealt with a white man one on one I was raped. You will not do this, or I will cut it off and feed it to the creatures of the night!

Don't let my appearance fool you, I am still a Native American woman and damned proud of it. If you are uncomfortable in my presence, say so. I have other things to do.

The true soul and true spirit of the tribes is, always has been and always will be the woman. The women of the tribes and the children of the tribes; they were the workers. If not for them, nothing would get done. Our men hunted; our men gave us protection. Many times these tasks took our men away from the women and children and the tribe, but the tribe endured.

The women of the tribes will continue to be the backbone and the spirit of the tribal family. Regardless of the outcome that is in store for Mother Earth and the people who live here, the women will endure. I am One of each Thousand, I have earned my place and I will keep it!

Your pale face weakens my stomach; I need a tea. The white man has always been as a wart on my ass, painful to sit on, painful to scratch and not too damned pretty to look at! Understand you, I have seen much. I have lived much. Nothing that I have lived as of yet has been palatable. I was murdered twice by the white man. I guess I didn't learn my lesson the first time. I came back to my people again to help, to care for the family, and to make the tribe strong.

My children at my side, I fought the Mexicans. I, at the side of my mother, fought the Texans. All the while I kept thinking, as I do today, "Goddamned white man! Who the hell does he think he is?" No one has ever provided me with an answer and I have asked that question over and over throughout my lifetimes. I deserve an answer!

What did my people ever do wrong? Fight to keep their lands free and pure. Fight to keep the waters pure. Fight to save our animals and our lands, which were our lives. Tell me now, Wolf!—if you can. My people were not regarded as lives; they were regarded as things—things that the other races that attacked us felt they could toss aside like a child's broken toy. I will not be trampled upon again. I am the knowledge now and I will have the wisdom. I am the scorn, the hate, and the remorse for all that has been done not only to me, but to all living things.

Who were these white men who felt that they could just come here and rape and maim and kill? What made them think that what was here for everyone should be theirs and theirs alone? There is a lesson in my history and the white man overlooks it purposely. I am called upon to teach you? How asinine and how degrading for me to have to remind the white man of what he has done to me. My tears are like blisters, they have come so often.

I am ugly inside and I have no control of my feelings. How I long to forget and to have love in my heart once more. But I am destined to these memories and as long as I must suffer their bitterness, I will share it with all.

I have no teachings for you white man; I have only revulsion for the vision of every white man. I will be cursed to carry the hatred until the One of each Thousand spirits for the last time. This is not fair; I have been cheated. You smile

140

at me and ask what I have to share with you. Why in hell did the white man not ask that question so long ago? We would have gladly shared, but the white man took, took, took. A slow and painful death to each of them in each of their lives. I wish that they all rot in the fires of the hell they have created for themselves.

See my ugliness. See my bitter hatred and know that this is not natural; this was done to me. Now leave my sight and never return. I loathe who you are; there are others more deserving. I disgust in what you represent; it is not fair.

Now that I have expressed my own bitterness, let me tell you a few things that you need to hear; I will reach atonement with my own pride for telling you later.

I must first tell you of your mother. No matter how horrible one can think his mother is, she meant well, as all mothers do.

The white man's respect for women, especially the mother, can be described as nonrealistic when compared to Native American ways. In my heritage the men of a tribe treated women with equality and recognized them for the part of the whole that they were. The white man looks down upon the women of his race. Many white women look down upon themselves as well. They may not outwardly reflect such actions, but the inner spirit is not pleasing. In the white man's society, women are discriminated against at work, in the home—everywhere. People pass laws that are aimed at preventing such things, but the laws are a waste of the paper they are written on. When women cannot be treated equally in a society, there is no respect, no oneness. The white man reveres himself above all others, above all things.

Mother Earth is a thing to the white man, something that exists to serve his purpose. The white man looks down upon Mother Earth the same way he looks down upon his women. When man looks down upon that which created him, that

141

which bore him, and has a lack of respect for that which is responsible for his very existence, then surely he is already dead, and I feel no guilt.

My Mother Earth has done nothing but give and give. She has no greed, no stipulations, no strings attached, but she does have needs and man has denied her those needs.

As we speak, one hundred percent of the waters of Mother Earth are suffering some sort of pollution. There is no river, no stream, lake, no ocean or sea that is untouched. You bastards dump your filth into her waters like she has the ability to just wash it away for you so you can keep doing it. It turns my stomach to think that the glass of water that I need to sustain my life, a glass of water that Mother Earth once gladly gave to me, was once your piss! Would you like to ask me again if I am bitter or should I just spit in your face now?

My people knew what they were doing. My people were following the Grand Creation. My people were untouched by the white man's hands and lived well, in harmony and in perfect balance with Mother Earth. But this was not good enough for the white man.

When the white man first came to this land, my people looked at him with curiosity; we did not know what to expect. My people were just as curious to see the white man as the white man was to see us. But with the white man came his answer to our curiosity; Murder! For a long time we were helpless against the guns and the calvaries. We watched as the white man killed our fathers, our brothers, our husbands. We watched as the white man raped and killed our women— at least my people were good for something in the white man's eyes. We watched as the white man slaughtered our buffalo in sport; and when that wasn't enough, he killed more of my people.

When my people fought back, the white man laid all blame on us. He called us savages! The white man's stories of "how the west was won" make me hang my head in pity for him. The real way the west was won required the mass genocide of a beautiful people, tribe by tribe. It is truly a wonder that there are any of us left. The tribe endures for a reason: Mother Earth has plans for us yet.

Now the white man is seeking our ways. Now the white man thinks maybe we had the right answers after all. Well it's just too damned late! You seek our trinkets, you write books—everything so beautiful. Beautiful because you describe our pain and you use our words. Hindsight is a real kick in the ass, isn't it?

If you remember nothing of my bitterness, remember this: The mother is the root of who you are and no other. Without the mother you would not be here. The same holds true for Mother Earth; without her there is nothing left for you. So keep right on spilling your poisons into her; it's too late anyway.

I am Red Hawk in Winter, One of each Thousand, true daughter of the Mother Earth. I answer to no one but myself.

White Deer and Falling Snow: Sisters of different Mother Earths whose paths crossed for the purpose of my "enlightenment." These guides took me to and from each of their Mother Earths, far and near, and presented me with the differences between their Mother Earths, that were so much alike, it was uncanny. Both my guides were not able to speak on the same Mother Earth. I learned that without their home soil, there was no energy to draw upon, no knowledge available, nothing they could share.

I am White Deer. I will bring you to tribes long since past. I will show you the peace that once was and its downfall.

I am pleased to have you visit my Ina, my mother. You will find that she will be most glad that you are upon her. She will welcome you and her people will welcome Ska Tashuunka Wakan, the White Wolf. Many of her people knew your father and told stories of his destiny and of his son who would one day come to them with a soul yearning to be filled. Your coming will give truth to the stories. He was a great Wichasha pejuta, a great healer sent forth to find the last tribe, the One of each Thousand.

You will see the true Lakol wicohan, the true Indian way, and you will benefit from its lessons, lessons you will not realize you have learned until they are put to good use.

Here you will reunite with your true Sicun, the part of your soul which sings your song, the part of your soul that is who you were, who you are, and who you will be.

I stood in a field of what must have been two hundred horses. None of them were tied up. There were no fences. It was as if they knew where they were supposed to be. They were not startled by my presence. Even as I touched them and though they looked me in the eye, their grazing continued.

In the not so far distance, smoke was rising from an

encampment. I could hear voices carrying on conversations in a language that was not English, but that I understood as if it were.

I could hear the voice of White Deer, but I could not see her. She encouraged me to enter my "home" and reunite with my "family." As I walked toward the camp, I could hear children's voices as they called out to the camp, "Tashuunka Wakan! Tashuunka Wakan!" The Wolf! The Wolf!

As I neared the camp, I gazed at the tents, tepees. They were dirty, but their markings and paintings told the stories of the people who lived in them, stories of great hunts, stories of great chiefs. I was greeted by an old man who grasped my arm in friendship and welcomed me into his circle. As we walked through the camp, all eyes were upon me. The voices said that I had strange skin, that I was without color. My clothing was the same as others' in the camp, but I was from another tribe. My new friend bowed slightly to everyone as we passed them in the camp.

We came upon a group of women who were cooking over three massive fires. Meat and hot stones covered with cakes. They were busy with their tasks but took a moment to acknowledge my presence.

As we continued to walk through the camp, we came upon a little girl who was busy with what appeared to be a small doll. I bent down to speak to her and she looked at me with a smile that took her entire face to create. She was a beautiful child. I took the doll from her hands to look at it more closely; it was a doll in the image of an Indian child. I noticed the doll did not have a face, eyes, or a mouth. I asked why the doll did not have a face and the little girl's reply clearly suggested that she was surprised I did not already know: *"She has not been born yet!"*

It was like a knife in my stomach that this little girl could touch me, move me with her innocence and her knowledge.

The little girl reached out and rubbed my arm, as if she was trying to wipe away whatever was on my skin that prevented me from looking like her. She told me that I must be someone special to be different. I felt that knife again. To think someone is special because they are different—a concept far beyond the time I was in.

I stood and turned toward my camp guide, but he was nowhere to be seen. White Deer was standing where he had been.

These are my people as the old ones knew them. They truly are a beautiful people, are they not? I nodded my head in acknowledgement. *Even this small child, one who must be innocent if only for her age, knows of the new life that lies ahead of her. She knows that there is more for her in her next life.*

I looked around the camp, engulfed in the vision of a people all going about their day, performing their tasks.

"I find this all hard to believe. I mean, that people get along in this manner. I hear only happy voices. Am I being shown a false picture?" I looked to White Deer for her answer. There had been a tone of sarcasm in my voice. Without warning, White Deer lashed out and slapped the side of my face with such a force, I was startled and my face stung from the blow.

Is that what you prefer? All that I tell you, all that I show you is truth. Why does your mind not allow you to believe what your eyes provide it? Why must you believe that your eyes are showing you something that is not there? There is no gain in my attempting to fool you; why would I try? These people are the indigenous ones of my tribe. They are my true beginning. You are noticeably different to them, but do they treat you so? None of these people have scorned you, turned their faces from you in disgust, feared you. These are an accepting people. They may know that you are different, but their hearts tell them that you are still the same as they are.

146

Do their warriors attack you? Do their chiefs proclaim you
evil? No! These are a perfect people in the eyes of one another.
Their lives are filled with hard work and difficult tasks, but
they perform them for the benefit of each other and none of
them will complain. This family exists as a whole; it exists for
the benefit of all. There is no "me" in this family, there is only
"we." Think of the benefits your Mother Earth could derive
from my Ina if all her children thought of themselves as part
of the "we" instead of the "me" that they now consider all
too important.

I heard White Deer's words and considered them quickly
but carefully. She was right; there was nothing wrong with the
picture I saw. The only problem was that it was a picture I was
not used to seeing and it was indeed strange to me. The people
were the same. These Indians were the same as those who first
began Mother Earth. Their names were the same, their faces
the same, their ideals and objectives the same. I can't describe
all that I saw in a good enough manner to show that it was like
a movie. It was like everything I had ever been taught or learned
about Indians, their heritage and cultures. It was too easy;
therefore, it was hard to believe.

How silly we are on our Mother Earth not to realize that
what we see is the truth, if we would only let our minds accept
it. But my people have a bad habit of trying to read into the
visual story what our imagination tells us must also be.

Falling Snow asks for your time. I will take you to her,
then be silent as the burial grounds. I will meet with you again
and show you what happens to these perfect people. Then
perhaps you will know the feeling of true tears, the pain of
their burn on the hearts of an entire people, not just your own.
Falling Snow will tell you of her tribes, who, unlike my family,
had different plans for their existence. Open your eyes wide,
Wolf. Miss nothing, believe everything; challenge your eyes,
but believe everything.

White Deer pointed to a direction behind me and I turned to look. There before me was Falling Snow, who must have been a thousand years old. I looked back toward White Deer, but she was gone.

Why do you look back? That knowledge is useless to you now. Come, look forward with me. Falling Snow took my hand in hers and we walked toward a giant forest. I could see only trees and had to look as high as my head could tilt back to see the sky.

You wonder of my age. Falling Snow had a kind of mischievous tone in her voice. *"I planted these trees,"* she stated emphatically. There was a twinkle in her eye that either meant she was pulling my leg or she was saying, "Stick that in your pipe and smoke it!"

So, you are he! You are not what I expected. I should add that I am not impressed, if that does not hurt the ego your people are so famous for.

This forest before us, it is as those before me who have stood strong, proud, never falling. My people were the warriors of my Mother Earth. We were the greed that was placed here with purpose. You call us renegades, but we were not renegades, not really, just ornery, like you! We do have obvious differences though. I believe my people had more inner spirit, more guts, more courage. It took you so long to get here and I do not understand. Waking up is a simple thing to do. You perhaps were not paying attention? No matter, you are here now and there is much to see, very much to see.

It seemed as though we walked through the woods for hours. Everything seemed to take a lot of time on my journeys, even though they lasted for a short time. As we continued through the forest, I began to hear the noises of an encampment. People's voices rising above the forest. As we approached the noises, I could see a camp, not unlike the one I had visited with White Deer. At the edge of the camp, I could see the faces of the people more clearly. They were not like White Deer's people at all. These people had painted faces, bright reds, blues, and yellows. They wore a lot of handmade jewelry and scant clothing.

As we began to walk into the camp, I was quickly approached by one of the warriors. He literally jumped in front of me and held a knife to my throat.

"The White Wolf is not welcome here!" he screamed. At that instant, Falling Snow grabbed the warrior's arm that held the knife to my throat and growled something to him that I did not understand. The warrior backed away and with a mighty scream ran off to join the others in the camp.

There was much activity in the camp. Not in performing tasks or anything like that, just a lot of movement by the warriors as they whooped and ran around in the camp. I looked at the faces of many of the warriors and all I saw, all I felt, was anger, great anger.

Falling Snow placed her arm in front of me to stop my progression into the camp. She then slowly waved her arm about the air.

We war today. Many will die, many of our own home, many. The warriors will move to steal the holdings of another camp, the food, the wares. A futile war of laziness, yes, that is what it is. I cannot even liken them to children, who in my mind are filled with a better spirit of mind. Yes, we will war today and many will die. My people do not care much for the hunt, unless it must be. Much easier to take from others. Here in this camp you will see the markings of many tribes. The women, the wares, all of another camp, all by another hand. What a lazy bunch; but they are my people.

Even now, in my time and in my place, you see that Mother Earth is using her children in order to keep our numbers at that which she can sustain. The times tell her the numbers and no other. Mother Earth is truly wise, sometimes wicked, yet truly wise. We are the tribe she has chosen to do her bidding; at times we may not like that, but this is so. My people know their role on Mother Earth and they perform their functions well. Are we a murderous breed? I think not. I catch myself foolishly questioning Mother Earth and the things that she does, but then I kick myself while realizing that I should not question her greatness. She knows for what she does.

I remember building the first war lodge of our tribe. All the peoples helped and yet very few knew of its purpose. My husband was Four Bears; he was a great chief and I was his woman. He knew of the purpose for the war lodge, knew that it was needed. The people asked no questions. I too knew of its purpose; I could see it in my husband's eyes.

Upon the completion of the war lodge, the words of my husband to the people were clear but were painful, even to a tribe such as mine: "Go forth and cleanse this, our Mother Earth, and do this that she asks without question. Those of you who return will be celebrated, those who do not, honored. If you be either of these people, know that you serve a purpose that is necessary and all in our hearts will be forgiven."

My husband was a wise man for a fool, but you will notice that I laugh when I say this. You see, my husband too went out with the warriors to cleanse our Mother Earth. He was one who we celebrated many, many times, then honored. My ritual was to die with my husband, but my mind would not let me do so. I led my people for a time until I too was honored. Honored not for wars, not for cleansing Mother Earth, but honored for what Mother Earth stood for, which I held deep in my heart and distributed freely to the hearts of my people.

We are not savages; we are people. We are those who were given the gift of life and used it as we believed it should be. We expressed our appreciation for the gift by asking no questions when the gift called upon us.

I remember the song of my sister as she guided me to the path of the dead, guided me to my place of rebirth. I live mortal now, elsewhere; you see me here as the warrior woman I once was. I hope the pride that I have in who I was, who I am, and who I know I will become does not frighten you, for the combination of the three totals a true beauty.

The gift I freely give to you is the gift of my words—small when compared to the gift you have received from Mother Earth. I am Falling Snow, One of each Thousand, true daughter of Mother Earth.

Falling Snow faded before my eyes, gone on to better places, or to give the gift of her words to others, I am sure. I was saddened to see her go.

As she faded I felt a hand on my shoulder. I turned slowly and found that White Deer had returned. She motioned to me with her hand to follow, and as I did we re-entered her camp. I looked back towards the camp of Falling Snow, but it was forest again, still beautiful, still tall.

Falling Snow is truly a gentle woman. She is set in her beliefs that they might give her comfort as she continues to question herself. I often find her to be too deep in recollection. I cannot expect her to let go of her past, but she has difficulty in realizing a future that must be.

You, Wolf, are a curious one. You follow those of us whom you meet and you remain still. I wonder that you may be too accepting, but I do not judge you.

The kindness of my family that you have seen has continued to this day, but there is a small problem. Those of us you see here represent all of us that went forth. We are too few against the many that exist on your Mother Earth. How do so few voices grasp the attention of so many ears, so many minds? I tell you how, we call upon the Wolf, and better to make them listen, we call upon the White Wolf.

Standing Wolf is a good friend to be chosen by; I hope

151

you are aware of this. Standing Wolf chooses his sons carefully and with much argument within himself. Take his hand, Wolf. Never let go. The lines you see in my face, they should be familiar, my smile the same as the last one you witnessed, my eyes the same. If you do not yet realize, then I will tell you: I am she who was once Falling Snow. I am the new life that tells a different story. I am she who has witnessed a tribe that changes, a people that calmed, and I share a vision of the past that carries me to where I am and to where I will go.

I hope you have learned the beauty of two different peoples who were once the same. True, I be all these people, but now I am Falling Snow, One of each Thousand, true daughter of the Mother Earth.

Roaring Bear: A son of Standing Wolf, I came to learn. Roaring Bear was a warrior who had no war. He was a proud man who revered his heritage, honored his people. He always had a look of concern on his face.

> *My father, and my father's father, you knew them, Wolf. They are not here now, but they are, for I am here, and so are you.*
>
> *You must take my hand for this journey and keep it tight. I will be your feet upon my Mother Earth. Though she welcomes strangers with open arms, I am ashamed to admit that I have a jealousy for her. The white man has never visited my Mother Earth before and of this I am glad. I understand your heritage, Wolf, but I fail to see through the color. If this be so, I will understand and I will speak with you anyway.*

Roaring Bear took my hand in his; the grasp was tight. He produced a white feather from a pouch about his waist and placed it on the back of my head where I can only assume it remained.

> *This gift I give to you was a gift from my father. It is the healing symbol and I have found that it carries great medicine. I saw its healing powers as they were passed to you in the Valley of the Sun, so I believe that you understand.*
>
> *I will not show you my people; I will not take you to my camp. A camp is a proud place, but it is where the women will take you as it is their domain, their touch with Mother Earth.*
>
> *I will show you instead my land. I will show you its beauty and its strength. I will show you how it once was because I know you have not seen such things before.*

We began to walk through a valley between mountains, more like large hills. The grass was green and very thick, like a carpet. There were wild flowers everywhere and butterflies that danced among them. There was a scattering of leafy trees, none too tall to block the miraculous view. One could see forever, it seemed. No pollution, no buildings, no noisy cars. If there was ever any doubt about why the Native Americans of my Mother Earth were so upset over the white man's coming, this sight alone proved it.

We continued to walk the land and in the distance I could make out a herd of animals, which I assumed were buffalo. A group of prairie dogs were busy about their borough just ahead of us. Birds soared through the air above our heads, not seeming to notice or to care that we were there.

A little further on our way, we came upon a brook. I immediately noticed how clear the waters were. I could see to the bottom and thought that it must not be very deep. Roaring Bear bent over and cupped his hand in the water. He drank several handfuls, then having had enough, motioned to me to do the same. I cupped my hand like my new friend had done, gathered up the water and drank. So many times I had heard the term *ambrosia* but never had anything to compare it to, until now. I drank several more handfuls and didn't want to stop until Roaring Bear tugged at my hand. He told me that if I didn't stop my sides would ache and I would slow up our journey. He told me that there were waters everywhere and that I would be able to drink of them again. I couldn't wait.

As we continued to walk, Roaring Bear said little. He, who lived in this place, still appeared to be as taken with its beauty as I was seeing it for the first time. I wondered what it would be like to live here permanently and it pained me to be shown something I could not have. Much like a child whose sibling teases him with candy, I felt as if I were being tormented. This was not fair; but then, I guess that was the point.

The grasping of your hand has allowed me to see this place through your eyes and through your mind. It was a great joy to behold my land through the eyes of one who is a stranger here. You truly enjoy all that you are seeing and I too am enjoying it with you.

On your Mother Earth, such land and such places are no longer in existence. Much building, many people, and much poisoning has taken place. I feel sorry for you and your people because of the time that they are in; they know not what they do not have. My people are right, the white man is his own punishment. Man is truly the only creature on Mother Earth who punishes the children who have yet to be born. I think, Wolf, that you were born at the wrong time, but I am told that I am mistaken.

My land is green, my skies are blue, and my waters are pure. Your land is brown, your skies are brown, and your waters are brown. Do you not tire of brown?

My people have love and respect for one another, my animals roam free, and my land belongs to all people. Your people murder each other, your people murder the animals, your people are murdering the land in their desire to possess it. What are they trying to possess? A land poisoned? A land covered hard with roads? A land that has been raped so often it can no longer bear fruit? Why must I bother with you? Why must you bother to bring my words to your people? Am I to believe that a people who have no respect for Mother Earth will care to listen to what I have to say? These questions of "why" that I ask are all answered in the same manner because like my people, and my people before me, I care and I love your people even though their faults number greater than all the generations before me.

I laugh within myself when I see the vision of your people in your mind. Their vision to venture away from Mother Earth, to travel to distant worlds. I wonder, should they find such a world, will they just throw their Mother Earth away? Will they abandon her, not having learned any lessons? Will they go to another world and do the same thing? Will they go to another world and poison its waters, dirty its sky and rape its land? I think your Mother Earth is correct in her heart in putting a

155

stop to all this before your people do find another world. Surely what your people desire is not what they deserve.

Look around you, Wolf, and reveal what you see. You see rocks, grass, trees, flowers, animals. It would take you forever to describe what you see, but I can describe it in one word. What I see is life. You have a curious song, Wolf, but no matter, it is your song. You have the right mind, one that questions and one that demands. If your people will truly listen, tell them what you have seen; tell them that you have seen life and that it was truly wondrous. I understand that it is too late for this message, but tell them anyway. Surely, if nothing else, your people deserve hope.

As you leave my side today, I know that you will not forget me and I will not forget you. I have spoken with your voice, I have thought with your mind, and I have seen with your eyes. You must let this beauty shine through; it is your song and to keep it within is truly curious.

I know you have the feeling within because I have the feeling within and I, like the brothers and sisters who have guided you before me, am the Wolf. Your indigenous roots have reached out to you in desperation and, like we knew in our hearts that you would, you have responded.

You take us with you and we keep you with us. Our strength, courage, wisdom, and love is that which will continue to guide you through even your unconscious thoughts. We always knew our life had meaning and you must know this, too. You are the last of our rebirth and are all that we truly believe. Never be afraid to reach out your hand, we will always be there to grasp it, like I grasp it now, with the strength of all of us before me, all of us before you.

Your song is my song, but you hesitate to sing it as I have. You keep it silenced within a heavy heart and you blame no one but yourself. This is not how I was; this is not how you were. Honor me and sing my song; I long to hear it once more.

Sleep well with these thoughts and know that they and the thoughts of each of us have meaning. Think no more that they are myth.

I am Roaring Bear, One of each Thousand, true son of the Mother Earth.

David Little Fox: A son of Standing Wolf. Little Fox was young, very young, perhaps fourteen or fifteen. He had shorter hair than most that I have traveled with and he was very agile. Looking at him was like looking at a picture. He was all I could see, everything else was darkness.

> ***Welcome, my brother. I am David Little Fox. My appearance to you is one of surprise, I can see. Do not let my age fool you, for I am much older than you and much wiser as well.***
>
> ***You do not fear the darkness that surrounds me; this is good. The darkness you see is like a great wall. It stands between where we are, at the edge of your time, and where we will go, to the time to come.***
>
> ***I am tasked to apprentice you with the knowledge of a future that will not be yours as you are now. I am tasked to bring you to the wisdom that will come. Keep close at hand and do not fall behind; I am your key to existence in the place that we journey to.***

With that the Indian boy turned away from me and disappeared into the blackness. I quickly followed as he had instructed. I did my best to keep close to him, but like I said, he was very agile. He moved as if he took steps but with a swiftness that said his feet did not touch the ground. I am not all that sure mine did either.

As the blackness began to quickly fade, I saw before me what appeared to be a massive desert. There were no trees, not a single cactus. A hazy sun shone high in the sky, but I could scarcely make it out. It was as if there was a thick fog hanging overhead. It appeared to be gray and in places black, like a rain cloud. Off in the distance I saw a lightning bolt strike the ground once, twice, and dance back and forth where it struck.

Little Fox stood next to me, looking at the lightning bolt as was I. His eyes filled with amazement at the sight.

Limited as it may be, it is life. This is the between land, the land that lies between what was and what will come. There is nothing here for you to see, really, except for the nothingness that in itself may be something.

I have waited a long time to show you this, Wolf, too long. You will not see the once great oceans here; they are gone. You will not see the once great cities; they too are gone. But most startling of all is you will encounter no other of your kind here; they are gone as well.

There are no animals, there are no trees, there are none of my people either. All of them gone and lost in a remembrance long since past.

There are no rules here; there are no laws. The air is thick with sickness, as it has been for thousands of years. The sun tries in vain to touch that which once thrived upon it, but the sickness has prevented it. If you could see through the sickness, you would see the sun weep, much as you are doing now.

There are no mountains here; they have humbled to the will of Mother Earth. There be no living thing here as far as the eye can see and as far as we could travel. All but the life contained in the bolts from the sickened skies has perished. But even the bolts might not be life. There are none to share it.

I see in your thoughts that you wonder why it is here to nothingness that we came. I bring you here to show you that there is something here. Something that you have been gently warned of but had yet to see. There be punishment here, Wolf.

My time with you is limited. I, unlike my brothers and sisters before me, have very little to show you and you have seen it. I have very little to tell you and I have spoken it, so I shall take my place away from you.

I am David, he who was Little Fox, One of each Thousand, true son of the Mother Earth.

Sara White Horse: Wife of Standing Wolf. Sara White Horse, like Red Hawk in Winter, was a modern Indian woman. She was not of my time but of a time just before me. She looked like a woman from the 1940s. Sara had gray and white hair and dark black eyes. She was small in frame and had very large hands. Her arms were crossed when we met and there was nothing I could see in her eyes. She wore very long earrings of beads in many colors, which was the only thing about her that had color. When I walked toward her, she met me with an immediate embrace.

Greetings, son of my husband. I have yearned to meet your face and see what my husband has become. I am pleased. I know you have seen many things in your journeys and it is with much happiness that I invite you to a gathering of great joy. A time of celebration among my people. Attend with me and witness my joining with my husband.

Sara turned me around by my shoulders to the vision of an encampment, much like those I had already seen, but this encampment was immense. At quick count I guessed there were a hundred tepees and five times as many people about the camp.

Great preparation was going on, I could tell. Everyone appeared busy with a task. There was a lot of cooking, lots of meat and vegetables. The children were busy decorating each other's faces and arms and legs with colored paints. A lot of laughter and talk could be heard. Something wonderful was going to happen.

In almost the center of the camp was the largest tepee of them all. It was brightly painted and decorated and many medicine shields and beaded decorations hung about it and on poles around it.

Off to one end of the camp, many men were gathered around another tepee where they appeared to be preparing for something. We entered the camp and not one person acknowledged our presence as we walked about. Sara's face was one big smile as she watched everyone going about their tasks.

Large pieces of meat were on the many fires on cooking sticks and the baskets set around were filled with corn and onions and what looked like beans.

This is my wedding day and all are taking part in its preparation. I am to wed the Chief today in a great ceremony. We have planned for this day since the winter snow and now the day has come. He who will be my husband is as happy as I for this day.

We entered the large tepee in the center of the camp. There an Indian woman was resting on her knees in front of an Indian man. She was dressed in a beautiful gown of leather and feathers and beaded jewelry. She wore a golden band around her forehead and golden bands around her arms and wrists.

The Indian man was chanting over her in a low tone. I could not make out what he was saying. This was curious since until now I was always able to understand the people in my journeys.

The Chief asks the great One to watch over her and to bring great things and many children to her life. He gives her his blessing for the joining to come and offers his hopes for a fruitful and happy life with her new husband.

I walked around them, looking at the bride's face. Sure enough it was Sara, but not the older Sara that I was with. She was a younger Sara and didn't seem to be more than fifteen years old—but certainly she must have been older.

We walked toward the other side of the camp to where the group of men were gathered. There was much laughing and what appeared to be the teasing of a man I could not see.

The groom makes ready to greet his bride as well. This too is a happy day for him. He will marry the daughter of the Chief and become Chief in doing so. The braves around him

161

hope to win his favor in their showing of pride at his pending marriage. They speak of pride and the great things they know he will do as Chief. He will win great battles and provide for the people through great hunts. They talk of his name being placed among the legends that have yet to be written.

I walked around and within the group of men as they helped to adorn the garments of the groom. As I walked around to get a better look at the groom, my eyes widened as he slowly came into view. He was Standing Wolf, not the ancient old Indian man I had met before, but the young warrior I met on the mountain, the young warrior who answered all my questions, the young warrior who saved my life. I was humbled in his sight. His robes of color, the adornments that had been placed upon him, and the wolf's headdress that he wore were stunning. He was tall and proud in his face. He had somewhat of a smile to his face but was definitely complacent. He raised his head, looked in the direction where I stood, though I knew he could not see me, and smiled a great smile and began speaking happily to the other men.

He feels your presence and he is glad you are here at his side. He is proclaiming to the others that the spirits are with him and that they, too, rejoice in his pending joining to the daughter of the Chief. He is telling them of his spirit to come who is with him this day, with him to witness the joining and to give blessings upon the bride and groom. The others are pleased that the spirits approve of the joining.

A massive whoop rose up from the people in the camp and the groom began to make his way toward the center of the camp; I knew it was time for the joining. The groom walked slowly, perhaps contemplating that which was to come, or their future together. He continued to have the complacent look on his face with an occasional grin as he walked. I walked at his side and I could not help but keep my eyes fixed upon him. This was the great man that would do much, not only for me, but for all people to come. I was truly humbled to attend his wedding, even though I could not physically be there.

As the people gathered in the middle of the camp, the groom stood about twenty feet from the opening of the great tepee. The old man I saw in the tepee came out first, followed by the bride. She was beautiful in her joining dress and kept her head bowed as she approached the groom.

The bride and groom took their places in front of the old Indian man as he began to speak not only to them, but to the entire camp.

He speaks of the duties that the bride and groom will have. He speaks of their responsibilities to their people and to the great family. He speaks of the Grand Creation and its meaning, and how it is responsible for this joining, and that this joining has purpose in the eyes of the One. He speaks of the future and the changes that will come at the leading hands of the bride and groom.

He speaks of the bride's responsibilities to her husband and he speaks of the groom's responsibilities to his wife. He tells of the love that they will share for one another and no other. He speaks of the strength that they will provide to each other and the confidence they will instill in all the peoples.

He speaks of the passing of the feather from the old Chief to the new Chief and how all the people should support the new Chief as he stumbles to lead them while he learns.

As the joining continued, the old man spoke for what seemed like hours. At the end of the ceremony, the Chief touched the faces of the bride and groom, then lifted his arms and eyes to the sky and in chant asked for the blessings of the One.

He lowered his arms, then reached to the back of his head and removed a beautiful feather, which he handed to the bride. She held the feather to her forehead for a moment, then presented it to her new husband. He, too, held the feather to his forehead, then returned it to his new wife, who then affixed the feather to the side of her husband's head.

The passing of the feather is the symbol of who the people are. It represents the simplicity of the Grand Creation and its medicine is very strong. The feather, now with my husband, tells the people that he is Chief; it tells the people that he will take care of them.

The symbolic feather has passed down from Chief to Chief, from Medicine Man to Medicine Man. The feather: its plumes of many represent the peoples and all are attached to a single stem—the One. From where we came, all will remember, as a great man of your time once said, "Until time and times are done."

Now it is time that we leave here and that the people leave you to yourself. It is time to return you to where from you came as your people need you now more than ever; their plumes have fallen from the stem.

I am Sara White Horse, true daughter of the Mother Earth, Mother of the One of the One of each Thousand.

Epilogue

It has been a long time now since my night travels. I miss them and often yearn for them to return. They were a great escape.

I came away from this experience with many lessons learned. The words of wisdom of many that I encountered are covered here. I think you will agree that they all had something to say that touches a person inside in some way.

While I was compiling this book, I had occasion to wonder whether or not my own interpretations of what these pages contained should be added. I have since decided that these writings are for the benefit of all and I am included. I feel it necessary that readers know how I interpreted much of the contents and I have tried to do that. As I have stated before, I am not a writer, but I do have opinions, boy do I have opinions!

The messages in this book should be clear to you by now; you didn't get this far and not reap something from these pages.

I am not afraid to tell you that much of what I interpreted this book to mean has set back my thinking a long way. I have been shocked (literally) and I may have been shocking. I have been insulted and I may have been insulting. I have felt that mankind on the whole has been attacked and I may have attacked. But when I sit back and soak in all that is in this book, I can only come to one conclusion: mankind deserves it all. Mankind deserves a swift kick in the ass for what he has done to Mother Earth and mankind itself.

I have a whole new respect for Mother Earth and the Native Americans. Likewise, I have a whole new disrespect for mankind and what mankind has done, myself included. I like to think I am more aware of things now, but I wonder. It took the events of the past year to get me to recycle, a simple procedure that I have never done before. It took me this long to realize that I was as much the cause of damage to our environment as everyone else. It took me this long to realize that one person does and can make a difference in our world.

By nature and upbringing, I am introverted. I used to care little about others and as long as others didn't bother me, I was fine. I did not take the time to survey my world and determine in my mind what was wrong with it. I was concerned locally and nationally. I pondered world events but not their meaning. I bitched about income taxes, government waste, the cost of living, and why it cost more to fill my trunk with groceries than it used to—the standard stuff. But I never really took a hard look at or gave an earnest thought about anyone else; I just didn't care.

The big difference today is that now I do care, but the caring attitude came too late. I still get pissed off to this day because I wasn't "woken up" a long time ago, a time when it would have mattered, done some good. It frustrates me that this book carries my name and preaches "love one another," among other things, because that is something I could never do in the past. Charmaine, God love her, has tried in vain to tear down the walls, but as with everyone else who ever tried to get close to me, I put my foot down and she gave up. This is not fair to her, nor is it fair to you. This is why I felt you should know I am no different than anyone else who is trying to get by. We have had generations of learning how to build walls, but no one has ever taught us how to tear them down when the time came.

When we are young it is "spare the rod and spoil the child" and when we get older it's the same crap only we call it "kick ass and take names later." Why do we live in a world where it is acceptable to beat the hell out of each other and kill each other? Why do we live in a world where somewhere, someone is *always* at war? Why do we live in a world where men try to dominate women and why must women have to try to outdo men, and the same battles between races, cultures? If nothing else I have learned that we are all equal, all one people. This is nothing more than a fifty-fifty shot we were given here on earth and no matter how even the odds, we keep screwing it up! How do you take people who were raised one way and get them to instantly change? You just can't do it; I don't care who you are!

At home I ask myself each election year: Why do we have politicians who verbally beat each other up, get dragged through the mud in the press, and spend millions of dollars to get elected to a job that doesn't even pay a fraction of what it cost to buy it? (Yes, buy it!) Don't tell me these men and women want the job so they can do some good for the people, because that's bullshit and we all know it. Scandal after scandal and there is always a lie to cover it up. Politicians always have their hands in someone's pockets. Why must we have a two-party system? Why can't we all stand for the same good?

Why do we live in a society where persons have such hate for each other? Why do women berate men and men berate women? Why do children grow up in a civilized society not knowing where they came from, their heritage, or the necessity of caring for their environment and the Mother Earth?

Why do we live in a society with people who strive for nothing more than to hold themselves above others, to be richer, to have more possessions, and to have more power? Why do these cruel people profess their belief in God and perform their deeds in His name? Do they truly believe that going to church once a week makes all the greed and all the hatred okay? They believe that a one God gives them their wealth and they instill their wealth with "In God We Trust."

Why are people so obsessed with money? Why must

money be so important? When time began people did without money. Why can't the world be a community? Why can't people work together for the benefit of each other? History and remembrance tell of only one people who did this, the Native Americans, and it was working until the white man came along and butchered them tribe by tribe.

This is not a scolding for today's people; we are innocent of the crimes of our ancestors. But sometimes I feel like our forefathers and our ancestors should be dug up and shot for their crimes against Mother Earth and her children. I don't want to hear from any flag wavers who want to tell me what a great country we have become in spite of our forefathers or because of what they did. I know the history of my country and it was built on rape and take. I love this country like everyone else and I have a deep respect for all that it has been through, but this does not mean that I or anyone else has to believe it was for the better. The people and the system that were here were far better than anything we have today. Sure, Native Americans had wars with each other and I am sure they had their faults, but when it came to preserving Mother Earth and having respect for her and all that she stood for, there is no comparison today.

All this is easy to sit back and ask, but the answers just aren't there. We all know the type of world we have created for ourselves, and those of us who realize that it must stop are powerless. Powerless against the money, powerless against governments, powerless against the armies, powerless against our own self doubt.

So, Mr. Big Mouth Book Writer, what are the answers? Well, I don't have the answers either or this book would have been short and sweet. However, I do have some suggestions and you can do with them what you will.

I firmly believe that the AIDS virus was created through chemical warfare experiments. I firmly believe that when it did not pan out, it was kegged and dumped into the oceans in hopes that it would go away. I firmly believe that trying to hide it didn't work and it was released into the waters and infected a select group of people, say the Haitians or the Africans. I firmly believe that the virus has slowly spread from there through tourists and other travel and has reached all parts of the earth and is continuing to spread. I firmly believe that the waters we depend upon are tainted with the virus and it will eventually afflict every man, woman, and child. I firmly believe that through the spread of this virus, man has signed his own death warrant. I firmly believe that all of the waters of the earth are now affected in some way and anything in them, the fish and other life, are affected and will succumb to the disease. Consuming anything from the waters will further spread the disease.

I firmly believe that all people must grow their own food.

I firmly believe that drilling for oil must stop.

I firmly believe that driving vehicles, flying planes, and any other form of transportation that pollutes must stop.

I firmly believe that all chemical production must stop. I firmly believe that all industry with polluting smoke stacks must come to a stop.

I firmly believe that all space travel must stop—and this one hurts.

I firmly believe that the production of nuclear weapons must stop.

I firmly believe that nuclear power plant construction must stop and those already in existence must be shut down.

I firmly believe that dismantling the nuclear weaponry in the Johnson Atoll will result in the deaths of millions of people and loss of millions of aquatic, plant, and animal lives.

I firmly believe that people all over this earth, from whatever country, must take control of their governments and weed out the diseased and greedy politicians.

I firmly believe that there is not a government on this earth that is not corrupt.

I firmly believe that the monetary systems of each country will fall in favor of a world currency.

I firmly believe that every man, woman, and child of this earth is financially and morally bankrupt.

I firmly believe that the day will come when it does not matter how much money you have amassed, it will be worthless.

I firmly believe that we are Mitakuye Oyasin, all one people. I firmly believe that it does not matter from where we came, what color we are, what our heritage is, and who our ancestors are, we are all responsible for what lies ahead and we must take control and accept responsibility.

I firmly believe that Mother Earth will strike back and destroy all living things on this earth. I also firmly believe that we deserve her wrath.

I firmly believe that we live again and again and that no matter how many times we try it, we just can't seem to get it right.

I firmly believe that after Mother Earth wipes out all living things, a select few will be given another chance, perhaps millennia down the road. I firmly believe this will be the last chance we get and we will at last get it right.

I also firmly believe that of those who are gifted with that last chance, none will be white, none will be black, none will be red. In fact all will be one beautiful color and there will be no room for bigotry or racism. All will be a caring people who will actually support one another and who will grasp a hand no matter whose it is if it needs help.

I firmly believe that these new people will be a deserving people who will know of their poisoned heritages and refuse to allow them to thrive again.

I firmly believe that people have been on Mother Earth longer than our so-called intelligent brains can comprehend.

I firmly believe that we are behind in the times we were once in for this go around in life.

I firmly believe that we once traveled to and from this planet and others freely with and without the aid of crafts.

I firmly believe that somewhere along the lines of rebirth evolution slipped and somehow we lost our good senses.

I firmly believe that I will return to this earth someday and it will be all I want it to be.

I firmly believe that peace and harmony are not words but actions and they will be practiced throughout the new world.

I firmly believe that each will be his own master and will perform the job well.

I firmly believe that governments and monetary systems will not exist and the people will be all the better for it.

I have never believed in religion but have always believed in the inner god.

I have always believed that I am in control of my destiny, that everything happens or does not happen for a reason.

I have always believed that all people are the same, that we are all equal; but like most of you, I fell into the niche of my peers.

I have always believed that good would triumph over evil, but only if it was meant to be.

Finally, I have always believed in my heart that somewhere, somebody out there loves me. And now I am able to say I firmly believe that I love you, no matter who you are.

I am Anthony Michael, One of the One of each Thousand, reborn son of Standing Wolf, reborn son of Sara White Horse. More important, I am the Wolf, now a true son of the Mother Earth.

Questions, comments, write to Anthony Michael, POB 5901, Security, CO 80911-5901. For a personal reply, include a self-addressed stamped envelope.